WHAT OTHERS ARE SAYING ABOUT JOHN WEBSTER AND THIS BOOK

"I've read countless books on spirituality, but this one stands out. John Webster's insights and practical advice have helped me cultivate a more compassionate and mindful approach to life.''

- Patrick Snow, Best-Selling Author of Creating Your Own Destiny

"John Webster's writing is engaging, witty, and full of wisdom. I thoroughly enjoyed reading this book and highly recommend it to anyone looking to explore Secular Buddhism."

- Dr. Heather DiBlasi, Addiction Psychologist, Professional Keynote Speaker, and Author of Understanding Addiction and Recovery

“JJohn Webster’s writing is relatable, witty, and full of practical advice. This book is a must-read for anyone interested in personal growth and spirituality.”

- Robin D. Lee, Author of Achieving Health and Longevity: The Artful Pursuit of Wellness and Vitality

“*Breaking Free from Religious Dogma* is a must-read for anyone who is tired of feeling trapped by their religious beliefs. John Webster offers a refreshing and empowering perspective on Buddhism that has changed my life for the better.”

- David Nguyen, Graphic Designer

“I've recommended this book to all my friends and family. John Webster has a gift for making complex ideas simple and relatable. The teachings of Secular Buddhism have helped me find more peace and contentment in my life.”

- Emily Chen, Marketing Manager

“John Webster is a gifted writer and teacher. *Breaking Free from Religious Dogma* is a comprehensive guide that is both practical and inspiring. I've learned so much from this book and am grateful for the wisdom it contains.”

- Kevin Lee, Product Manager

“As a therapist, I often recommend *Breaking Free from Religious Dogma* to my clients. John Webster's approach to Secular Buddhism is grounded in compassion and self-awareness, and the book has helped many of my clients find greater peace and happiness.”

- Jennifer Smith, Licensed Therapist

“I've read many books on Buddhism, but *Breaking Free from Religious Dogma* is one of the best. John Webster's writing style is engaging and relatable, and his teachings have helped me find more meaning and purpose in my life.”

- Alex Brown, Freelance Writer

“John Webster's book is a breath of fresh air. His approach to Secular Buddhism is practical and relatable, and this book has helped me find more peace and contentment in my life. Highly recommended!”

- Rachel Kim, Software Developer

“*Breaking Free from Religious Dogma* is a gem of a book. John Webster's teachings on Secular Buddhism are insightful and empowering. These philosophies have helped me find greater joy and fulfillment in my life.”

- Maria Hernandez, Financial Analyst

“John Webster's book is a game-changer. It has helped me see Buddhism in a whole new light and has provided me with practical tools for living a more mindful and compassionate life.”

- Jonathan Lee, Attorney

"*Breaking Free from Religious Dogma* is a must-read for anyone interested in Buddhism. John Webster's teachings are grounded in wisdom and compassion, and this book has helped me find greater peace and happiness in my life."

- Erica Lee, Yoga Instructor

"John Webster's book is a true gift. His teachings on Secular Buddhism are accessible and inspiring, and his book has helped me find more meaning and purpose in my life."

- Jessica Martinez, Sales Manager

"*Breaking Free from Religious Dogma* is an excellent guide for anyone seeking a more fulfilling way of life. John Webster's teachings on Secular Buddhism are practical and relatable, and his book has helped me find greater peace and happiness."

- David Wilson, HR Manager

"John Webster's book is a must-read for anyone interested in Secular Buddhism. His teachings are grounded in compassion and self-awareness, allowing me to find more joy and fulfillment in my life."

- Katherine Lee, Consultant

"*Breaking Free from Religious Dogma* is a life-changing book. John Webster's teachings on Secular Buddhism have helped me find more peace and contentment in my life. This book has inspired me to be a better person."

- Mark Thompson, Mechanical Engineer

"I've read many books on Buddhism, but *Breaking Free from Religious Dogma* stands out. John Webster's teachings are practical and relatable. This amazing book has helped me find more meaning and purpose in my life."

- Melissa Chang, Registered Investment Advisor

"John Webster's book is a must-read for anyone seeking a more mindful and compassionate way of life. His teachings on Secular Buddhism are accessible and inspiring. I have been able to find greater peace and happiness."

- Alex Kim, Entrepreneur

"Beautiful and empowering book. John Webster's teachings on Secular Buddhism are grounded in wisdom and compassion, giving me more joy and fulfillment in my life."

- Jessica Lee, Artist

"John Webster's book is a true gem. His teachings on Secular Buddhism are practical and inspiring. Applying the principles has helped me find more peace and contentment in my life. Highly recommended!"

- Matthew Davis, Biochemist

EXPLORE A NEW SPIRITUAL PATH AND BREAK FREE FROM THE CONSTRAINTS OF RELIGIOUS DOGMA!

BREAKING FREE
FROM RELIGIOUS DOGMA

EXPLORING SECULAR BUDDHISM FOR PERSONAL GROWTH

JOHN WEBSTER, MBA

Pinacle Peak Press
New York, NY

Breaking Free from Religious Dogma
Exploring Secular Buddhism for Personal Growth

Published by:
Pinnacle Peak Press
New York, NY

Now, if you want to get in touch with me about ordering more copies, booking speaking engagements, or maybe even a round of golf (I could use the practice), here's the number: (480) 500-8500. You can also shoot me an email at John@CoachJohnWebster.com or check out my website at www.CoachJohnWebster.com (it's like a virtual retreat, but without all the mosquitoes).

ISBN: 978-1-962043-07-6

Editors: PublishingDoctor.com
Cover Photo: Shutterstock.com

First Edition, First Printing 2024
2 3 4 5 6 7 8 9 10

DEDICATION

Alright, folks, it's time to get a little sappy. This one's for the important people in my life.

First and foremost, a big shoutout to Richard Olin Webster, Sr. (1944-2021): My dad was a true legend, with a positive mindset that could light up a room. He taught me everything he knows about entrepreneurship, motivation, and the power of relationships. We're talking about a guy who truly believed that anything was possible if you were willing to work for it. He may be gone, but his legacy lives on.

Next up, my mom, Helena: She brought me into this world and taught me some important skills along the way. And let's not forget all the positive words of encouragement. I love you, mom!

And of course, we can't forget about the kids. Caleb, Brianna, Jacob, Emma, Leopold, and Scarlett: You're the reason I wake up every morning ready to take on the world. I hope you'll benefit from the message in this book, and I want you to remember that you can create your own future.

Last but not least, we have to give a shoutout to my beautiful wife, Melissa: She's been there for me through thick and thin, supporting my entrepreneurial endeavors and being my best friend and soul mate. We're talking about a love that's divine and complete, people!

And to all the future generations out there, I've got a message for you. Even though you haven't met me yet, I'm coming at you as a voice from the dust to teach you everything I know.

Finally, we can't forget about you, the reader. It's an honor and privilege for me to be your mentor and coach. I'm here to help you transform your life and achieve your wildest dreams. Let's do this!

ACKNOWLEDGMENTS

It's time for some shoutouts! I want to recognize and thank all the people who have supported me, encouraged me, and believed in my dreams. And let's not forget about all the folks who have helped me along the way, providing motivation and inspiration. You guys are the real MVPs!

We're talking about friends, family, mentors, coaches, teachers, and maybe even a random stranger or two. You know who you are, and I want you to know how grateful I am for your help.

You've made my life richer and stronger, and I wouldn't be the person I am today without you. So go ahead, give yourself a pat on the back. You deserve it!

And if you're reading this and you're feeling a little left out, don't worry. I appreciate you too. Without you, I wouldn't be where I am today. So, thanks for being awesome!

CONTENTS

INTRODUCTION:

Breaking Free from Religious Dogma (with a Twist of Humor)

Welcome, my fellow seekers of truth and enlightenment! Are you tired of feeling like your religious beliefs are holding you back? Are you searching for a way to live a more fulfilling life without sacrificing your values? If so, then you're in the right place.

You see, I used to be just like you. I was a lost soul wandering aimlessly through life, searching for meaning and purpose. But then, one day, I discovered the power of Secular Buddhism, and my life was never the same.

Now, I know what you're thinking: "Buddhism? Isn't that the religion with all the chanting and incense and bald guys in orange robes?" Well, my friend, you're in for a surprise. Secular Buddhism is a whole new ballgame.

Instead of focusing on religious dogma, Secular Buddhism offers practical techniques for mindfulness, compassion, and self-awareness. It's like the stripped-down, non-denominational version of Buddhism, with all the good stuff and none of the baggage.

But let's back up a bit. Why should you care about Secular Buddhism in the first place? Well, let me tell you a little story.

Once upon a time, I was a devout follower of a certain organized religion. I won't name names, but let's just say it rhymes with "Hristianity." (Okay, fine, it was Christianity. Happy now?)

Anyway, I loved my religion. It gave me a sense of community, purpose, and meaning. But over time, I began to feel like something was missing. I didn't agree with some of the teachings, and I felt like I had to suppress my true self in order to fit in with the group.

I tried to ignore these feelings, but they just kept getting stronger. And then, to make matters worse, I had a several traumatic experiences, some with leaders of the church, some from horrible actions from family members, some from contradicting doctrines, and some from dealings of life itself. It was like all the flaws and limitations of the religion were staring me right in the face.

I was lost, confused, and disillusioned. I didn't know where to turn. And then, one day, I stumbled upon Secular Buddhism.

It was like a ray of sunshine breaking through the clouds. Suddenly, I had a new spiritual path that aligned with my values and sense of self. I learned how to cultivate mindfulness, compassion, and self-awareness, and I felt like I was finally living a more fulfilling life.

And that's what this book is all about. It's about breaking free from the limitations of religious dogma and finding a new spiritual path that resonates with you. Whether you're a seasoned Buddhist or just curious about exploring new spiritual paths, this book is the perfect guide to help you find meaning and purpose in a secular world.

But first, let's talk about why so many people are turning to Secular Buddhism in the first place.

Religious dogma can be a powerful force in people's lives. It offers a sense of community, purpose, and meaning that can be hard to find elsewhere. But for many people, religious beliefs can also be limiting and even damaging. They may feel like they have to conform to a set of rules or beliefs that don't align with their values or sense of self.

Moreover, some people may have experienced trauma or abuse within religious institutions, leading to a distrust of organized religion altogether. In these cases, the need for a new spiritual path that offers the benefits of religion without the drawbacks is all the more urgent.

So, what are some of the specific drawbacks of religious dogma? Here are a few that you may have experienced yourself:

- The feeling of being trapped or constrained by religious beliefs or practices.
- The pressure to conform to a set of rules or beliefs that don't resonate with your values or sense of self.
- The fear of being ostracized or shunned by your community if you deviate from religious norms.
- The trauma or abuse that can occur within religious institutions, leading to a loss of trust or even hatred of organized religion.

Secular Buddhism offers a way to break free from these limitations and find a new spiritual path that aligns with your values and sense of self. By focusing on practical techniques for mindfulness, compassion, and self-awareness, Secular Buddhism can help you cultivate a more fulfilling way of life.

In the following chapters, we'll explore the teachings of Secular Buddhism in depth, offering practical advice and techniques for living a more mindful, compassionate, and self-aware life. We'll also address common questions and misconceptions about Buddhism and offer insights and guidance for integrating its teachings into your daily life.

So, are you ready to break free from religious dogma and explore the world of Secular Buddhism? If so, then let's get started on this exciting journey toward personal growth, fulfillment, and happiness. Let's explore the world of Secular Buddhism together, with a healthy dose of humor and a sprinkle of irreverence. I promise you won't regret it.

CHAPTER 1

Embarking on the Mindful Journey of Secular Buddhism

A Lighthearted Stroll Through Buddhism's Evolution: From Time-Tested Traditions to Modern Makeovers

Buddhism, one of the world's oldest and wisest spiritual paths, hails from India circa sixth century BCE. But like a fine wine, it's only gotten better (and more complex) with age. Let's take a whimsical walk through its transformation, from its traditional roots to its contemporary incarnations:

Traditional Movements:

Theravada Buddhism: Also known as "The Classic," Theravada is the granddaddy of all Buddhist schools. It's all about personal enlightenment and liberation, so if you're a solo spiritual traveler, this might be the one for you!

Mahayana Buddhism: The cool older sibling of the Buddhist world, Mahayana emerged a few centuries after Theravada and has more sub-schools than you can shake a dharma stick at! Zen, Pure Land, Nichiren—you name it, they've got it. Mahayana's all about enlightening yourself and others, so if you're a team player, this might be your spiritual squad.

Vajrayana Buddhism: The mysterious cousin, Vajrayana is also known as Tantric or Esoteric Buddhism. With origins in India, it migrated to Tibet and Mongolia, bringing with it meditation, ritualism, and visualization. A bit more complex, but hey, who doesn't love a good puzzle?

Modern Movements:

Engaged Buddhism: The activist of the family, Engaged Buddhism emerged in the latter half of the 20th century as a response to things like war, injustice, and environmental crises. Engaged Buddhists believe that Buddhism should be put into action, not just meditation. So if you're into spiritual activism, this one's got your name written all over it!

Secular Buddhism: The practical prodigy, Secular Buddhism rose to prominence in the 21st century, mainly in the West. It takes a no-nonsense approach to Buddhist teachings, ditching supernatural elements like karma and rebirth for more down-to-earth wisdom. If you're into Buddhism without the mystical mumbo jumbo, this might be your cup of Zen tea.

Western Buddhism: The cultural chameleon, Western Buddhism is all about adapting traditional Buddhist practices to fit in with Western culture. This has led to new forms like Insight Meditation (Vipassana), Mindfulness, and Vajrayana practices, with a Western twist. So if you're looking for something closer to home, this one's for you!

Conclusion:

Buddhism, like your favorite sitcom, has evolved over the years, keeping up with the times and taking on new forms. With traditional movements still going strong and fresh, modern approaches sprouting up, there's never been a better time to take a lighthearted leap into the world of Buddhism!

The Secular Buddhism Starter Pack: Mindfulness, Meditation, and Non-Attachment for the Modern Spiritual Seeker

Secular Buddhism, the no-nonsense approach to ancient wisdom, is all about putting Buddhist teachings to work in our everyday lives. So, let's get down to brass tacks and dive into the key principles: mindfulness, meditation, and non-attachment.

Mindfulness is like having a personal mental detective, helping you become more aware of your thoughts, emotions, and physical sensations without judgment. Think Sherlock Holmes, but for your inner world. By observing your mind, you'll discover all sorts of fascinating patterns and habits you never knew you had.

Meditation is your personal chill pill. By focusing on something simple, like your breath or a mantra, you're training your mind to be calm and clear. It's like hitting the "reset" button on your mental browser, so you can better understand the interconnected web of life.

Non-attachment is the art of letting go without actually letting go. Confused? Don't worry! It just means you can enjoy life and relationships without getting too attached, because everything is subject to change. It's like enjoying a beautiful sandcastle at the beach without getting upset when the tide washes it away. Embrace the impermanence, and you'll find life's a lot less disappointing.

Mindfulness, meditation, and non-attachment are the three amigos of secular Buddhism. By practicing these principles, you'll find inner peace, clarity, and a compassionate approach to life. Plus, you'll be the life of the (spiritual) party!

Traditional Buddhism vs. Secular Buddhism: A Lighthearted Comparison of the Spiritual Heavyweights

Buddhism, like a spiritual buffet, offers a little something for everyone, with its two major branches: Traditional Buddhism and Secular Buddhism. Let's take a look at their differences and similarities, so you can decide which flavor of Buddhism satisfies your spiritual taste buds.

Beliefs:

Traditional Buddhism is all about the teachings of the original Buddha, who's like the spiritual CEO. Here, the focus is on enlightenment and deities, including the Buddha himself. It's like a cosmic quest for the ultimate spiritual truth.

Secular Buddhism, however, is more of a humanistic approach. Think less cosmic quest, more self-help book. The focus is on personal growth and living a peaceful, fulfilling life without the need for deities.

Practices:

Traditional Buddhism revolves around monasteries, where monks and nuns meditate and study like spiritual superheroes. They take vows of poverty, chastity, and obedience, all in pursuit of the ultimate prize: Nirvana.

Secular Buddhism is less monastery, more meditation app. It's an individualistic approach centered on living a mindful, aware life. Secular Buddhists see meditation as a key tool for self-improvement, not just a means to reach Nirvana.

Differences:

The main difference between these two spiritual titans is the focus on spirituality. Traditional Buddhism is all about reaching enlightenment, while Secular Buddhism sees spirituality as a bonus that comes with living in the present moment and understanding one's thoughts and feelings.

Traditional Buddhism also treats the Buddha's teachings as sacred and unquestionable, while Secular Buddhists see them as a source of inspiration and guidance for personal growth—not a set of rigid dogmas.

Similarities:

Despite their differences, Traditional and Secular Buddhism have some common ground. Both value meditation and mindfulness, as they bring inner peace and clarity. They also emphasize self-awareness and compassionate living, which help us navigate life's ups and downs.

In conclusion, whether you're drawn to the spiritual quest of Traditional Buddhism or the down-to-earth approach of Secular Buddhism, both offer valuable insights and practices. So go ahead, dig in, and enjoy your spiritual feast!

Science Meets Secular Buddhism: When Mindfulness and Lab Coats Collide

In secular Buddhism, science is like the trusty sidekick, helping to explore the mind-body connection, psychology, and neuroscience. Secular Buddhism favors a rational and empirical approach to spirituality, using scientific research as a map for navigating the mind's mysterious landscape.

The mind-body connection is the dynamic duo of secular Buddhism, showing how mental states and physical states are joined at the hip. Scientific studies reveal that our thoughts, feelings, and reactions have a direct impact on our physical health and well-being—like a cosmic dance between mind and body.

Psychology lends a hand in secular Buddhism, too. Practices such as mindfulness meditation, compassion training, and cognitive restructuring have received the scientific stamp of approval. These techniques have been shown to help with emotional regulation, stress reduction, and overall well-being. It's like having a mental first-aid kit, backed by science!

Neuroscience is the brainy cousin in this secular Buddhist family. Research on meditation and mindfulness has unlocked the secrets of the brain, showing that these practices can reshape our gray matter and promote neural plasticity (that's brain-speak for adaptability). The brain is like a muscle—meditation is its gym.

In a nutshell, science plays a starring role in secular Buddhism, especially in understanding the mind-body connection, psychology, and neuroscience. By marrying science and spirituality, secular Buddhism offers a powerful toolbox for navigating life's complexities and finding inner peace.

Secular Buddhism Tackles Social Justice: Ethics, the Environment, and Activism with a Dash of Humor

Secular Buddhism is like the practical cousin of traditional Buddhism, focusing on the Buddha's teachings with an emphasis on self-reflection, mindfulness, and compassion. Secular Buddhists roll up their sleeves and dive into ethical perspectives and social justice issues, championing causes like environmentalism and social activism.

When it comes to environmentalism, secular Buddhists are all about that interconnectedness and interdependence. Picture the natural world as a giant game of Twister, with everything intertwined and reliant on each other. So, when environmental degradation strikes, it's like a tumble in the Twister game, affecting the environment, humans, and other living beings alike.

Secular Buddhists are like the eco-warriors of Buddhism, promoting reduced carbon footprints, conservation of natural resources, and protection of biodiversity. They're the ones holding signs at environmental protests, signing petitions, and supporting political candidates who are as green as a leafy salad.

But wait, there's more! Social activism is another issue near and dear to secular Buddhists' hearts. They believe in getting their hands dirty to improve society and protect vulnerable communities. Guided by ethical principles like loving-kindness, compassion, and non-violence, secular Buddhists fight for justice, equality, and fairness for all.

From combating poverty to tackling discrimination and human rights violations, secular Buddhists are on the front lines, supporting community-led movements and grassroots campaigns that put vulnerable communities in the spotlight. They're the ones engaging in conversations with policymakers, pushing for systemic change and transformation like true social justice superheroes.

In a nutshell, secular Buddhism brings ethics and social justice issues, such as environmentalism and social activism, to the forefront. With mindfulness, meditation, and ethical reflection as their trusty tools, secular Buddhists are on a mission to create a more equitable and just society for all, one compassionate act at a time.

Meet the Secular Buddhist All-Stars: Notable Teachers and Their Contributions to the Movement

Stephen Batchelor: Think of him as the poster boy for secular Buddhism! A former monk turned author and founder of the Bodhi College in Europe, Batchelor brings secular Buddhist teachings to the masses. His books, like Buddhism Without Beliefs and Confession of a Buddhist Atheist, have become modern classics, and he's known for making Buddhism relatable for skeptics and spiritual seekers alike.

Martine Batchelor: A former Zen nun turned British teacher, Martine is all about incorporating mindfulness and compassion into everyday life. Her book titles say it all, like Let Go: A Buddhist Guide to Breaking Free of Habits, and The Spirit of the Buddha. She's a master at helping people turn daily routines into spiritual practices.

Noah Levine: From punk rocker to meditation teacher, Levine founded the Against the Stream Buddhist Meditation Society in Los Angeles. He's the Johnny Rotten of the secular Buddhist world, advocating for a "radical dharma" that addresses social justice issues. With books like Dharma Punx and Against the Stream, he's not your average meditation teacher.

Tara Brach: As a clinical psychologist and meditation teacher, Brach blends mindfulness-based approaches to psychotherapy and personal growth. She's the founder of the Insight Meditation Community of Washington, DC, and the author of life-changing books like Radical Acceptance and True Refuge. If you're looking for inner peace and freedom, Tara Brach is your go-to teacher.

Sharon Salzberg: A loving-kindness guru since the 1970s, Salzberg has been a prominent figure in the Western Buddhist world for decades. She's the co-founder of the Insight Meditation Society in Massachusetts and the author of inspiring books like Lovingkindness and Real Happiness. If you want to open your heart and feel the love, Salzberg's teachings are a must.

In a nutshell, these secular Buddhist superheroes have contributed immensely to the movement, championing mindfulness, social justice, and practical Buddhist teachings. Their collective goal? To spread understanding and compassion worldwide, helping people lead meaningful and fulfilled lives one mindful breath at a time.

Practical tips and advice for incorporating secular Buddhist practices into daily life

Practical tips include starting a meditation practice, cultivating mindfulness, and living in the present moment. Set realistic and achievable goals for your practice. Begin with short meditation sessions, and gradually increase the time as you become comfortable.

Practice mindfulness in everyday life. Pay attention to your breath, sensations, and thoughts as they arise. Be present in each moment and try not to allow yourself to become distracted by the past or future.

Cultivate compassion and gratitude. Take time to reflect on the blessings in your life and extend kindness to yourself and others.

Journal about your experiences. Writing down your thoughts and reflections can help you to gain insight and deepen your practice.

Connect with a community of practitioners. Seek out like-minded individuals who can offer support and guidance on your journey.

Take time for self-care. Allow yourself to rest and recharge as needed and prioritize activities that bring you joy and fulfillment.

Be patient with yourself. Remember that progress takes time, and that the journey is more important than the destination.

Seek out resources and guidance. Read books, attend workshops and retreats, and seek out teachers who can offer guidance and support as you embark on your path.

Establish a consistent meditation routine. Try to meditate at the same time and place every day, even if it's only for a few minutes. This consistency will help you build a strong foundation for your practice.

Bring mindfulness into daily activities. Practice mindful eating, walking, or even washing dishes by fully engaging with the experience, focusing on the sensations and being present in the moment.

Embrace impermanence and non-attachment. Recognize that everything is constantly changing, and cultivate a mindset of non-attachment to outcomes, possessions, and relationships to reduce suffering and increase inner peace.

Develop active listening skills. When conversing with others, practice being fully present and attentive, letting go of the need to plan your response or judge their words.

Cultivate loving-kindness (Metta) meditation. Regularly practice sending love and compassion to yourself, loved ones, acquaintances, and even difficult people in your life to develop a more compassionate and empathetic mindset.

Engage in acts of kindness and service. Volunteer your time or contribute to causes that align with your values, and practice generosity in your daily interactions.

Practice non-judgmental awareness. Observe your thoughts and emotions without labeling them as good or bad, and then learn to accept them as they are without trying to change or control them.

Reflect on the interconnectedness of all beings. Understand that your actions have an impact on others and the environment, and then make conscious choices to live ethically and responsibly.

By incorporating these tips and advice into your daily life, you can begin to cultivate secular Buddhist practices that will help you develop mindfulness, compassion, and inner peace. Remember, this is a lifelong journey, and progress will come with time, patience, and consistent practice.

CHAPTER 2

Discovering the Delightful World of Secular Buddhist Principles

Secular Buddhism: The Laughing Buddha's Guide to Life Without the Fluff

Secular Buddhism is like the cool cousin of traditional Buddhism—keeping the wisdom but ditching the dogma. It's perfect for folks from any background who want to tap into the teachings of Buddhism without feeling the need to bow, chant, or wear robes (unless, of course, that's your style).

Imagine the core concepts of Buddhism as a groovy playlist that anyone can groove to, regardless of their religious beliefs or spiritual inclinations. Secular Buddhism cranks up the volume on mindfulness, compassion, and wisdom while giving a polite "no, thank you" to the rituals and practices that might make some folks feel like they've stumbled into the wrong party.

Instead of sticking to ancient traditions, Secular Buddhism is all about remixing the teachings for modern times. It tackles 21st-century challenges like the never-ending parade of smartphone notifications, the great divide between the left and the right, and the daily race against time.

At its heart, Secular Buddhism is like a spiritual life-hack, helping you become the best version of yourself, one mindful and compassionate step at a time. So, if you're ready to experience the life-changing power of Buddhism without getting bogged down in religious specifics, Secular Buddhism is your ticket to a more peaceful, fulfilling existence.

The Dynamic Duo: Mindfulness Meditation and Critical Inquiry, Secular Buddhism Style

Ever feel like your thoughts and emotions are throwing a wild, out-of-control party in your head? Enter mindfulness meditation, the superhero of Secular Buddhism, swooping in to help you regain control and find inner peace.

Mindfulness meditation is like a personal trainer for your mind, helping you flex your awareness muscles and focus on the present moment. As you practice, you'll learn to observe your thoughts and feelings without judgment, and give them a friendly wave as they pass by. The result? Less confusion, anxiety, and frustration, and more compassion, awareness, and acceptance—no religious beliefs required.

But wait, there's more! Critical inquiry is the trusty sidekick to mindfulness meditation. By questioning our assumptions and beliefs, we transform ourselves into mental detectives, uncovering new perspectives and deepening our understanding of the world around us. It's like Sherlock Holmes meets Secular Buddhism, helping us break free from our own biases and prejudices and consider all the possibilities.

Together, mindfulness meditation and critical inquiry form a dynamic duo that powers a secular Buddhist approach. They help us cultivate wisdom, acceptance, and compassion, giving us the tools we need to navigate life's complexities with grace and balance. So, put on your cape (or just sit on a cushion), and start practicing these superpowered skills today!

Secular Buddhists' Guide to Living in the Now: Dance Like No One's Watching

Secular Buddhists have cracked the code to living a fulfilling life: just live in the present moment, and let it all hang out! It's all about diving into the "now" like it's a pool on a hot summer day, soaking up every thought, emotion, and sensation without getting clingy or judgmental.

Think of it like dancing at a party. Secular Buddhists encourage you to dance like nobody's watching, without worrying about past missteps or future choreography. Just feel the beat and let the music move you.

Part of this groovy approach involves letting go of attachments and aversions. Imagine your favorite ice cream flavor—yum! But if you cling to that delicious, melty goodness too tightly, you're bound to end up with a sticky mess. The same goes for life. Embrace the impermanence of things, and you'll find greater peace and contentment.

Likewise, don't be the person at the party who's always complaining about the music. Reacting with aversion just leads to more suffering. Instead, try cultivating an attitude of non-judgmental acceptance and compassion. You'll not only alleviate your own suffering but also help others find their groove.

In a nutshell, Secular Buddhists believe that true happiness and fulfillment come from living in the present, free from attachments and aversions, and embracing compassion and acceptance. So, crank up the tunes, and let's dance our way to a more peaceful and contented life!

The Secular Buddhist Triple Treat: Four Noble Truths, Eightfold Path, and Three Universal Truths—Now with Extra Laughs!

If you're a fan of secular Buddhism, get ready to dig into its triple-layer cake of foundational principles: the Four Noble Truths, the Eightfold Path, and the Three Universal Truths. These sweet delights offer a recipe for personal transformation and spiritual growth that's simply too delicious to resist!

First up, the Four Noble Truths, which give us the lowdown on suffering and how to break free from it. They're like a self-help manual for the soul. They are essential principles in Buddhism that describe the nature of suffering and the path to liberation from it. They provide guidance for personal transformation and spiritual growth:

Dukkha: Suffering exists. Life is a roller coaster of suffering (but we've got the safety harness).

Dukkha acknowledges that suffering is an inherent part of life. It encompasses physical pain, emotional distress, and the fear of loss, illness, or death. The Buddha taught that dukkha arises from our attachment to desires and expectations, as well as our ignorance of the true nature of reality. By understanding impermanence, cultivating compassion and wisdom, and letting go of attachments, we can transcend suffering and attain true peace and happiness.

Samudaya: Suffering arises from craving and attachment. Cravings and attachments are like spiritual junk food—tasty but unsatisfying. Samudaya explains that suffering arises from craving and attachment, which cause us to cling to desires and become emotionally invested in them. Our attachment to desires can lead to negative emotions and a cycle of suffering. To overcome this suffering, the Buddha taught the importance of developing mindfulness and understanding the true nature of desires and attachments, allowing us to let go and experience greater peace and contentment.

Nirodha: Suffering can be overcome. Good news! We've got a suffering "off" switch, and it's called mindfulness. Nirodha offers hope by teaching that suffering can be overcome through mindfulness and the cultivation of compassion and kindness towards ourselves and others. This process of transformation leads to greater understanding, acceptance, and love, making us more compassionate, joyous, and connected to the world around us.

Magga: The path to the end of suffering is the Eightfold Path, which is a spiritual GPS to guide you out of Sufferingville. The Magga, or Eightfold Path, is the practical guide to ending suffering and attaining enlightenment. It consists of Right Understanding, Right Intention, Right Speech, Right Action, Right Livelihood, Right Effort, Right Mindfulness, and Right Concentration. Through the practice of the Eightfold Path, we cultivate virtue, concentration, and wisdom, enabling us to navigate life's challenges with clarity and compassion, and ultimately attain inner peace and happiness.

In summary, the Four Noble Truths provide a framework for understanding the nature of suffering and the path to liberation. By following these principles and practicing the Eightfold Path, we can achieve personal transformation, spiritual growth, and enlightenment.

Speaking of the Eightfold Path, it's the practical guide to achieving liberation from suffering. It includes:

1. **Right Understanding: Know the rules of the game (a.k.a., the Four Noble Truths).**

Right Understanding is the first step towards enlightenment in the noble eightfold path of Buddhism. It refers to having a correct understanding of reality that removes our ignorance and delusion. Right Understanding involves the realization that suffering exists, the root cause of suffering, the cessation of suffering, and the path that leads to the cessation of suffering.

Right Understanding is an essential component of Buddhism as it helps one develop a proper view of life. It teaches that the materialistic reality is temporary and that everything is constantly changing. Life is impermanent, and clinging to things leads to suffering. Failing to understand this concept leads to ignorance, which is the primary cause of suffering.

The correct understanding of the Four Noble Truths is at the core of Right Understanding. The first Noble Truth is that life involves suffering. The second states that the root cause of suffering is craving, which leads to attachment and clinging. The third Noble Truth affirms that suffering can be overcome, and the fourth Noble Truth presents the path to the cessation of suffering.

Having this understanding enables individuals to see life differently, embrace change, and live in harmony with the world regardless of its nature. It helps individuals to relinquish their attachment to material things, let go of their ego, and find peace within themselves. They accept the reality and work for the betterment of self and society, without attaching themselves to results.

In conclusion, Right Understanding is the foundation of Buddhist teachings. It is the key to seeing reality as it is, freeing oneself from suffering, and achieving enlightenment. With a clear understanding of the Four Noble Truths, one can develop a sense of compassion and empathy for all living beings and work towards a more peaceful world.

2. Right Intention: Set your spiritual compass to "enlightenment."

Developing the intention to follow the path is a crucial step in pursuing a spiritual or personal growth journey. To cultivate this right intention, one must first have a clear understanding of what their ultimate goal or aspiration is. For some, it may be enlightenment, while others may seek to simply live a more meaningful life.

Once the goal is established, it is essential to reflect on the reasons behind it. One must ask themselves why they want to follow this path and what motivates them. This introspection enables individuals to understand their true intentions and whether they align with their goal.

It is also important to acknowledge and overcome any hindrances that may prevent one from following this path. These hindrances may include fears, doubts, or distractions that can lead one astray.

To further develop the intention to follow the path, individuals can seek guidance and support from spiritual leaders, mentors, or communities. Engaging in regular practice and self-reflection can also strengthen this intention.

Ultimately, developing the right intention to follow the path is a continuous process that requires patience, perseverance, and dedication. By cultivating this intention, individuals can move closer towards their aspirations and live a more fulfilling life.

3. Right Speech: Use your words like a warm, fuzzy blanket.

Right speech is a fundamental part of living a moral and ethical life. It involves speaking honestly, kindly, and with good intentions, while avoiding harmful and hurtful speech. The power of our words can have a significant impact on others, and therefore it is our responsibility to use them wisely and compassionately.

Speaking honestly means being truthful, but it is important to use tact and sensitivity when delivering difficult news or opinions. We can express our feelings and ideas without being aggressive, confrontational or degrading towards others. We should also avoid gossiping or spreading rumors that have no basis in fact.

A key element of right speech is kindness. This means speaking with empathy, compassion, and respect towards others, even if we disagree with them. We should strive to be mindful of others' feelings and avoid causing unnecessary harm. Before speaking, we should ask ourselves whether our words are necessary, kind and true.

In addition, right speech should always have good intentions. It should be directed towards the welfare and benefit of others. We should refrain from using language that aims to hurt, manipulate, or control others.

Right speech is about balancing honesty with kindness and mindfulness, in order to build understanding and connection with others. When we use our words wisely, we can create deeper relationships, foster trust, and promote harmonious communities.

4. Right Action: Be the good egg you know you can be.

Right action is an essential principle in Buddhism that emphasizes the importance of acting ethically and virtuously towards all living beings. It advocates for a life that is founded on kindness, compassion, and respect for all forms of life. This principle is firmly rooted in the Four Noble Truths and the Noble Eightfold Path, which outlines the way to enlightenment and liberation.

Right action requires us to act in a manner that avoids causing harm to others. It encourages us to refrain from killing, stealing, and engaging in any form of unethical or immoral behavior. It also advocates for the cultivation of kindness and compassion towards all living beings, including animals, insects, and plants. This principle teaches us to treat others as we would like to be treated and to consider the consequences of our actions before we act.

In everyday life, right action can manifest in various ways. For instance, it can be seen in the way we treat our family, friends, and colleagues. We should act with honesty, integrity, and fairness and avoid causing harm or distress to others. Furthermore, we should extend the same level of respect and compassion to those we do not know, including strangers and individuals from different cultures and backgrounds.

Ultimately, right action is about living a moral and ethical life in harmony with the teachings of Buddhism. It is a way to cultivate inner peace and happiness while also contributing positively to the lives of others. Through practicing right action, we can become better individuals and contribute to a world that is more compassionate, kind, and just.

5. Right Livelihood: Make a living while making a difference.

A Right Livelihood encompasses the idea of earning a living that does not harm or exploit others. It is an ethical and sustainable way of making money, which takes into consideration the well-being of people and the planet, rather than just focusing on profit.

In order to achieve a Right Livelihood, one must have a deep understanding of the impact of their actions on society and the environment. They must seek out opportunities that align with their values and principles, and actively work to create positive change.

There are many ways to practice Right Livelihood, including working in fields such as sustainable agriculture, renewable energy, non-profit organizations, and ethical investment. Additionally, individuals can support ethical businesses, consume consciously, and reduce waste to promote a sustainable economy.

Ultimately, living a life of Right Livelihood requires a commitment to one's values and a willingness to take action towards a more just and sustainable world. By making intentional choices about how we earn and spend money, we can contribute to a better future for all.

6. Right Effort: Exercise those mindfulness muscles.

Cultivating positive mental states and reducing negative ones requires a conscious effort to regulate our thoughts and emotions. This process is known as Right Effort in Buddhism and involves developing a clear understanding of the nature of our mind.

To cultivate positive mental states, we need to start by identifying the negative ones that we want to overcome. Examples might include anger, anxiety, and depression. Once we have identified these negative states, we can work towards replacing them with positive mental states such as joy, compassion, and calmness.

To do this, we need to focus our attention on positive thoughts and actions. We can practice gratitude by reminding ourselves of the good things in our lives, and we can engage in acts of kindness, which can help us develop a more positive outlook. Meditation and mindfulness practices can also help us cultivate positive mental states.

Reducing negative mental states requires a similar approach. We need to become aware of our negative thoughts and emotions and work towards replacing them with more positive ones. This might involve challenging negative beliefs or engaging in activities that help us relax and reduce stress.

Overall, cultivating positive mental states and reducing negative ones requires a sustained effort. It requires us to be aware of our thoughts and emotions and to actively work towards developing more positive ones. With practice, we can gradually transform our mindset, leading to a more positive and fulfilling life.

7. **Right Mindfulness: Live in the now, not on your smartphone.**

Right Mindfulness is the practice of being fully present in the moment with a non-judgmental awareness of what is happening around us. It involves paying close attention to our thoughts, emotions, and sensations while we remain fully grounded in the present experience.

With Right Mindfulness, we learn to observe our thoughts without getting caught up in them. We become aware of our emotions without letting them overwhelm us. We acknowledge our physical sensations without reacting to them. Through this practice, we gain a deeper understanding of ourselves and our surroundings, and we become better equipped to navigate the challenges that life presents.

By approaching every moment with openness and curiosity, we begin to see the world in a new light. We notice the beauty and wonder of everyday experiences, and we are free to engage in life fully and authentically. With this kind of mindfulness, we can embrace each moment as a gift, and we can cultivate a greater sense of peace and joy in our lives.

So, let us all strive to practice Right Mindfulness in our daily lives. Let us stay present in each and every moment, observing our thoughts and emotions with non-judgmental awareness. By doing so, we can find true fulfillment and meaning in our lives, and we can live with greater intention, purpose, and happiness.

8. Right Concentration: Meditate your way to mental mastery.

Right Concentration is a crucial aspect of the Noble Eightfold Path in Buddhism. It is defined as the development of an unbroken focus of the mind, allowing us to stay focused and alert to our experiences without being distracted or affected by external stimuli.

Developing Right Concentration requires a disciplined and focused mind. One must make a commitment to maintain deep levels of concentration, and consciously avoid distractions that could disrupt attention. To achieve this level of focus, one might begin by practicing meditation, which is a powerful tool to calm the mind and cultivate focus.

The art of meditation involves sitting in a comfortable and quiet place, with eyes closed, and focusing on a particular object such as the breath or a mantra. The purpose of this focus is to bring the mind back to a single point and develop the ability to maintain that focus for extended periods of time.

Over time, practitioners may start to feel more aware of their thoughts and emotions, and begin to detach from them, focusing instead on a sense of calm and inner peace. This ability to maintain a state of concentration provides numerous benefits including improved memory, creativity, and problem-solving skills, as well as a greater sense of peace and relaxation.

Ultimately, developing Right Concentration requires discipline, practice, and patience. However, the rewards are transformative, as it allows for a greater sense of clarity and focus in our daily lives. By developing an unbroken focus of the mind, we can experience a sense of inner peace and tranquility, as well as improve our ability to engage with the world around us.

Alright, folks! Let's wrap up this spiritual burrito called the Noble Eightfold Path, served hot and fresh in the flavorful world of Secular Buddhism. It's got everything you need to get rid of that pesky suffering and attain a shiny, brand-new state of spiritual enlightenment. So, buckle up and prepare for a ride on the Eightfold Express to Nirvana Town!

The Eightfold Path is like a road map to enlightenment, carefully designed by the Buddha himself. It's the spiritual equivalent of a GPS that doesn't lead you into a lake, and it's got turn-by-turn directions to help you avoid life's potholes (and let's be honest, we've all hit a few).

What makes this path so groovy is that it's open to everyone—no matter your beliefs, background, or favorite pizza toppings. The Noble Eightfold Path is the ultimate self-improvement guide, complete with everything from a psychological tune-up to tips on how to land a righteous job that doesn't hurt Mother Earth.

Now, you might be thinking, “This sounds great, but can I really reach enlightenment while still enjoying Netflix and a cold beverage on a Friday night?” And the answer is a resounding “Yes!” Secular Buddhism is all about finding that sweet spot between ancient wisdom and modern living.

So, what are you waiting for? It’s time to hop on the Eightfold Path, ditch the suffering, and ride off into the sunset of enlightenment. Just remember, when it comes to Secular Buddhism, it’s all about the journey, not the destination. And who knows? You might even pick up a few laughs and make some new friends along the way!

Get ready to laugh your way through the Three Universal Truths, the heart of the cosmic comedy called life. They might sound serious, but trust me, they’re a riot when you dig deep!

Anicca: Impermanence - Life’s Never-Ending Game of Musical Chairs.

Imagine the universe as an enormous game of musical chairs, where everyone and everything is continuously shifting around, and nothing stays the same. That’s Anicca, the hilarious truth that nothing lasts forever. It’s like trying to take a selfie with a melting ice sculpture - good luck, buddy!

From mountains eroding to that pint of ice cream mysteriously disappearing from the freezer, impermanence is everywhere. Even our thoughts and emotions are fleeting, like trying to hold onto a soapy water balloon. This cosmic joke is a reminder that nothing lasts forever - not even the latest TikTok dance trend.

By appreciating the beauty of life’s constant changes, we can free ourselves from the suffering of attachment. So next time you’re feeling down, just remember: life is like a yo-yo, constantly going up and down, so buckle up and enjoy the ride!

Dukkha: Suffering - The Cosmic Prankster Strikes Again!

Dukkha is the cosmic prankster of the universe, leaving banana peels for us to slip on and constantly hiding the remote. Suffering is as much a part of life as popcorn at the movies or accidentally stepping on a Lego. It comes in all shapes and sizes, like that pesky mosquito buzzing in your ear at night.

Embrace the Dukkha! Realize that life's challenges are like a cosmic gym membership for your soul, building those spiritual muscles of empathy and resilience. The more you work out, the stronger you become!

Remember, how you respond to suffering is your choice. You can either be the laughingstock of life's comedy club or become a stand-up comedian, transforming your pain into laughter and growth.

Anatta: The Absence of a Permanent Self - The Ultimate Identity Crisis.

If you think your identity crisis in high school was bad, wait until you hear about Anatta! The universe decided that having a permanent self was too mainstream, so it went for the indie approach: no permanent self or soul at all!

Anatta is the ultimate plot twist: the self is a collection of temporary, interdependent parts, always evolving and changing like a kaleidoscope. Who needs a permanent identity anyway? You're a limited-edition masterpiece, constantly evolving!

By recognizing Anatta, we can let go of our attachment to the "self" and enjoy the ride of existence. After all, life is just one big cosmic rollercoaster, so sit back, hold tight, and enjoy the twists and turns!

Together, these Universal Truths are like the punchlines of life's biggest jokes. Embrace the impermanence, find humor in suffering, and let go of the illusion of a permanent self. Just remember, life is a cosmic comedy - so laugh along and enjoy the show!

The Three Universal Truths are like the cherry on top of our secular Buddhist cake. They remind us that life is:

Impermanent: Everything changes, just like that half-eaten cake in your fridge.

Unsatisfactory: Life's got its ups and downs, but that's what makes it interesting.

Non-self: We're all interconnected, so let's spread some love and kindness.

So there you have it! The Four Noble Truths, the Eightfold Path, and the Three Universal Truths: the fundamental Buddhist principles that secular Buddhists embrace with gusto. Dive into this triple treat and enjoy a journey of laughter, learning, and spiritual growth. Bon appétit!

Karma: The Cosmic Boomerang of the Mind in Secular Buddhism.

Karma - it's like a boomerang that whacks you on the head when you least expect it. In Eastern religions, this concept has long been tied to the whole "what goes around, comes around" idea. But in secular Buddhism, karma gets a facelift and a whole new interpretation.

Forget the mystical mumbo-jumbo! Secular Buddhism ditches the cosmic scoreboard and views karma as a psychological phenomenon. It's all about how our actions shape our noggin and influence our experiences, like painting a mental picture with the strokes of our choices.

Karma in secular Buddhism isn't about leveling up in the cosmic video game or dodging punishment in future lives. It's about understanding that our actions have a direct impact on our well-being and the well-being of those we interact with.

Picture this: when we act with kindness and compassion, it's like planting a happiness tree that blooms in our minds and relationships. On the other hand, when we act with anger or selfishness, it's like releasing a swarm of pesky, emotional mosquitos that buzz around us, causing distress and damaged relationships.

In this version of karma, the focus is on cultivating responsibility for our own emotional garden and engaging with the world with skill and compassion. It's less about a celestial carrot and stick approach and more about self-improvement and growth.

By paying attention to our actions and their ripple effects, we can become more mindful and intentional in our choices. So, let's whip out our psychological boomerangs and cultivate a more harmonious and fulfilling life!

Secular Buddhists: Interconnectedness, Compassion, and Ethical Shenanigans.

In the realm of secular Buddhism, you'll find folks who practice Buddhism free from religious trappings or supernatural hijinks. At the heart of their philosophy lies the understanding that all living beings are connected like a cosmic puzzle, with each piece relying on the others for survival and well-being. It's not just about humans, either—animals, plants, and even tiny microbes are part of this universal jigsaw.

Secular Buddhists also appreciate the importance of compassion, generosity, and ethical conduct in their daily lives. Compassion is like a warm, fuzzy blanket of empathy and concern for others, serving as the foundation for all Buddhist teachings. Generosity, meanwhile, is all about giving selflessly to others without expecting anything in return, like planting seeds of interconnectedness and unity among all living beings.

Then there's ethical conduct, a cornerstone of secular Buddhism. It's all about living according to Buddhist precepts, which are essentially a recipe for respect, kindness, and compassion towards all living beings. Key ingredients include avoiding harming others, lying, stealing, and engaging in any hanky-panky that might cause harm.

In a nutshell, secular Buddhists recognize the interconnectedness of all living beings and aim to cultivate compassion, generosity, and ethical conduct in their daily lives. These values are essential for fostering harmony, peace, and well-being, not just for themselves but also for the world around them. And isn't that just a marvelous way to live?

Secular Buddhism: Living the Good Life, Sans the Supernatural

Secular Buddhism takes the ancient wisdom of Buddhist teachings and gives it a modern twist, free from religious dogma or supernatural hocus-pocus. It's all about transforming Buddhism into a practical life philosophy that helps us understand our own minds and reduce suffering. But don't be fooled—this isn't just an intellectual exercise; it's a way of life that can revolutionize our experiences.

Secular Buddhism zeroes in on mindfulness, compassion, and impermanence like a laser. It teaches us that suffering stems from our attachments, aversions, and blissful ignorance of reality. By honing our mindfulness skills and keeping an eye on our thoughts and emotions, we can get a sneak peek into our true nature and the world around us.

Meditation and mindfulness are the bread and butter of Secular Buddhism. These practices help us develop a deep sense of awareness and presence, allowing us to tackle life's daily curveballs with grace and clarity. We learn to be more accepting, compassionate, and grateful, both towards ourselves and others.

But wait, there's more! Secular Buddhism doesn't stop at personal enlightenment; it acknowledges our interdependence with others and the world. It nudges us to cultivate compassion and sprinkle kindness and generosity in our interactions, fostering positive change and social well-being.

In a nutshell, Secular Buddhism is far more than just an intellectual pursuit or abstract idea. It's a practical philosophy and a way of life that paves the way for greater peace and happiness. By embracing mindfulness, compassion, and wisdom, we can overcome suffering and live a more joyful, fulfilling existence. And who wouldn't want that? It's a path toward personal and social transformation, creating a more just, peaceful, and sustainable world for all.

CHAPTER 3

Easing Your Way into Understanding the Nature of Suffering

The Hilarious Misadventures of Suffering: A Secular Buddhist Stand-Up Routine

Suffering, ah! That unavoidable guest at the dinner party of life. It comes in all shapes and sizes: physical, emotional, psychological – you name it, suffering's got it covered. So, let's take a deep dive into the philosophical and psychological roots of this all-too-familiar companion.

Philosophically speaking, suffering has been quite the celebrity topic. One classic conundrum, the Problem of Evil, had theologians and philosophers scratching their heads for centuries. If there's an all-powerful, all-good God, why on Earth is there evil and suffering? Some say it's because of human sin (thanks, Adam and Eve), while others claim it's just part of life's package deal.

Now, psychology offers a different flavor for understanding suffering. We've got external events like trauma, loss, or that time you accidentally waved back at someone who wasn't waving at you (ouch). Then there are the internal factors, like our ever-helpful negative thoughts, emotions, and behaviors. Enter the cognitive model: the idea that our thoughts about experiences dictate our emotional reactions. So, if you think you're a worthless potato because you failed at something, you'll feel as blue as a potato in a Picasso painting.

Philosophy and psychology occasionally have a rendezvous, like when existential philosophers (looking at you, Sartre and Heidegger) ponder the inescapable nature of suffering in human existence. Likewise, humanistic psychologists like Maslow and Rogers emphasize the significance of meaning and self-actualization as antidotes to suffering.

At the end of the day, understanding suffering's philosophical and psychological roots gives us the tools to ease its grip on our lives. By recognizing the intricate, multi-layered nature of suffering, we can approach it with empathy, compassion, and a readiness to unpack its underlying causes and meanings. And maybe, just maybe, we'll find a way to laugh in the face of suffering, Secular Buddhist style!

Suffering's Comedy Club: Physical and Emotional Dimensions on Stage

Picture suffering as a two-sided coin: on one side, we've got the physical woes, and on the flip side, we've got the emotional rollercoaster. Let's take a closer look at these show-stopping aspects of life's most challenging performance.

Physical suffering is like a pesky stagehand that can't help but trip the actors. It includes the likes of pain, illness, and injuries that turn our bodies into a scene from a tragic play. Chronic conditions, cancer, arthritis - all make us want to yell "cut!" and demand a rewrite. And as if the physical challenges weren't enough, they often drag their emotional sidekicks into the mix, causing depression, anxiety, and social isolation.

Now, let's talk about emotional suffering - the drama queens of the suffering world. Traumatic events, divorce, job loss, or the heartbreaking final act of losing a loved one can all lead to emotional anguish. And don't forget about mental health disorders, like depression and anxiety, which can steal the spotlight and bring the entire performance to a screeching halt.

The physical and emotional dimensions of suffering are like two performers in a pas de deux, each influencing the other. A sore back can lead to a grumpy mood, while emotional turmoil can cause headaches and muscle tension.

To bring down the curtain on suffering's theatrics, it's essential to address both its physical and emotional dimensions. We can offer our bodies a standing ovation through medication, therapy, or other medical interventions, while we applaud our emotional health with counseling or mental health support.

As we work on both fronts, we might just transform our suffering-filled stage into a feel-good musical.

In the end, life's playbill may be full of physical and emotional suffering, but by understanding and addressing these dimensions, we can make it a lighter and more enjoyable show, with a touch of Secular Buddhist humor, of course!

Suffering's Variety Show: Illness, Trauma, and Loss Walk into a Bar

Suffering, that universal experience, comes in an array of forms like a quirky variety show. With headliners like illness, trauma, and loss, we're in for quite the performance. Knowing the different causes of suffering can help us master the art of dealing with it. So, let's take a look at the star-studded lineup of life's most challenging acts.

Illness: Imagine illness as a stand-up comedian who doesn't know when to quit. With acute, chronic, and life-threatening gigs, it's got a little something for everyone. Physical pain, mental distress, emotional turmoil – it's like a three-ring circus of suffering.

Trauma: Next up is the unforgettable performance of trauma. Its repertoire includes abuse, violence, sexual assault, and natural disasters – a real showstopper, impacting not only the main character but also their supporting cast of friends and family.

Loss: Last, but not least, we have the ever-present loss, the drama-filled monologue of life. Loss takes center stage when we say goodbye to loved ones, jobs, or relationships, leaving us with emotional pain that can morph into depression, anxiety, or other psychological disorders.

Of course, suffering's variety show doesn't stop there. We've got side acts like poverty, discrimination, and environmental degradation, each with its own unique flair. The causes of suffering are as diverse and complex as a theatrical ensemble, and everyone experiences them in their own way.

In the end, recognizing the different forms and causes of suffering is like reading a playbill before the show. It prepares us to understand, manage, and cope with suffering, allowing us to offer support and resources to those who need their pain alleviated.

Suffering's International Comedy Tour: Culture's Impact on Personal Experiences

Cultural attitudes toward suffering are like stand-up comedians from around the world, each with their unique style, punchlines, and delivery. Just like comedy, our understanding and handling of suffering is colored by the culture we're from, affecting how we define, express, and cope with it.

In one corner, we have cultures that see suffering as the headliner of life's comedy club. They believe in toughing it out, cracking jokes with a straight face, and embracing stoicism. For them, self-sacrifice is the name of the game, and the ability to endure suffering is like winning the "Best Comedian" award.

On the other side of the stage, we have cultures that believe in a more improv-style approach to suffering. They emphasize overcoming pain and adversity and encourage seeking relief and resolution like it's a punchline waiting to be delivered. Here, just enduring suffering would be akin to bombing on stage.

Our cultural comedy styles impact our personal experiences of suffering. Picture a stoic comedian, raised in a culture that values toughing it out, hesitating to seek help or share emotions. They might struggle to understand or connect with other comedians who wear their emotions on their sleeves.

Meanwhile, the improv comedian from a culture that encourages problem-solving might treat suffering like a temporary setback, actively seeking help and support. However, they could feel the pressure to resolve their problems faster than the speed of a one-liner, making long-term healing and recovery a challenge.

In the end, cultural attitudes towards suffering can be as diverse as a comedy festival lineup. Acknowledging and understanding these attitudes helps us find ways to navigate our pain and adversity while staying true to our values and beliefs. After all, laughter might not be the best medicine, but it sure helps us embrace our suffering with a smile.

The Laugh Track to Coping: Mindfulness, Therapy, and More

Suffering is like the sitcom of life: sometimes predictable, sometimes unexpected, but always present. When faced with hardships that make us feel like we're stuck in a never-ending laugh track, it's essential to find coping mechanisms that keep the humor alive while helping us manage our suffering. Mindfulness and therapy can be the dynamic duo in this comedy of life.

Picture mindfulness as the straight man in our comedic routine. It's a meditation style that teaches us to stay present and focused without judgment, keeping our attention on the here and now. By doing so, we can steer clear of negative thoughts and emotions, and instead, embrace the sitcom of life without being overwhelmed or consumed by it.

Therapy, on the other hand, is like that hilarious friend who's always there to talk things out. With the help of a trained professional, we can dive into our thoughts and feelings, identify the root causes of our suffering, and learn new coping strategies. Together, mindfulness and therapy can be a powerful one-two punch against suffering.

But let's not forget the rest of the ensemble cast in our comedic lives. Other coping mechanisms like exercise, creative pursuits, and social support can help us manage our suffering too. Exercise is like a high-energy sidekick, helping us combat anxiety and depression. Creative activities, such as writing, painting, or music, can be like the quirky character that brings a sense of purpose and fulfillment to our lives. And social support, from friends, family, or support groups, can be like the warm and comforting laugh track that reminds us we're not alone.

In the end, life's sitcom is filled with ups and downs, but with a strong lineup of coping mechanisms like mindfulness, therapy, exercise, creative pursuits, and social support, we can keep the humor alive and manage our suffering, ultimately leading to a fulfilling and meaningful life. After all, laughter is the best medicine—or at least, it's a great coping mechanism.

Spirituality: The Cosmic Stand-Up Routine to Make Sense of Suffering

Spirituality is like a cosmic stand-up comedy show, with the universe cracking jokes and humans trying to find meaning and purpose in the punchlines. When life hands us lemons in the form of suffering, many people turn to spirituality to make lemonade, or at least laugh a little while they do.

Spirituality is a vast concept, but at its heart, it's about connecting with something bigger than ourselves, like a higher power, our inner Jedi, or the universal comic genius. This connection can offer comfort and hope when life hits us with a pie in the face.

One of the ways spirituality helps us find meaning in suffering is by offering solace through practices like prayer, meditation, or interpretive dance-offs with the cosmos. Whatever the method, spirituality can be a soothing balm during challenging times.

In addition to comforting us, spirituality also helps us find purpose in our suffering. It's like watching a stand-up comedy special where we realize the punchlines are actually life lessons in disguise, making us more compassionate, empathetic, and ready to take on the world.

And let's not forget the connection to others that spirituality can bring. Many spiritual traditions are like comedy clubs, where everyone gathers to laugh, learn, and grow together. This sense of belonging and purpose can be a real lifesaver during tough times.

However, it's essential to recognize that not everyone can find meaning or purpose in their suffering through spirituality. We all have our own spiritual journey, and just like comedy, what resonates with one person may not work for another.

In summary, spirituality can be like a cosmic stand-up routine that helps us find meaning and purpose in suffering. By providing comfort, hope, and connection, spirituality can help us laugh our way through life.

The role of community and social support in alleviating suffering

The importance of community and social support in alleviating suffering cannot be overstated. Humans are social creatures, and our connections with others play a vital role in our mental, emotional, and physical well-being. In times of suffering, the support we receive from our friends, family, and community members can have a profound impact on our ability to cope and heal.

One example of the power of community support can be found in the story of Sarah, a young woman who was diagnosed with a rare and debilitating neurological disorder. As her health declined, Sarah found herself increasingly isolated and unable to participate in her usual social activities. This loneliness only compounded her emotional distress and sense of hopelessness.

However, as her story spread through her community, people began to rally around her, organizing fundraisers to help cover her medical expenses and offering emotional support through visits and phone calls. This outpouring of love and solidarity not only provided Sarah with the financial means to access the necessary treatments but also gave her a renewed sense of hope and belonging.

Similarly, the experience of David, a single father who unexpectedly lost his job, highlights the role of social support in alleviating suffering. As David struggled to make ends meet and provide for his family, he was overwhelmed by feelings of anxiety, shame, and despair. Recognizing his need for assistance, friends and neighbors stepped in to offer help in various ways, from providing meals and childcare to assisting with job searches and connecting him with local resources.

In both of these cases, the involvement of community and social support networks made a significant difference in the lives of those who were suffering. These examples emphasize the vital role that community and social connections play in helping individuals navigate difficult periods and find the strength to overcome adversity.

To foster communities that are more compassionate and supportive, we must prioritize building and maintaining strong social connections, both in our own lives and in the lives of those around us. This includes reaching out to those who may be struggling, offering a listening ear, and connecting them with resources that can help. By doing so, we can create a world in which suffering is met with empathy, understanding, and a helping hand.

CHAPTER 4

Tickling Your Heart with Compassion and Empathy for Self and Others

The Art of Hugging Yourself: Self-Compassion as the Secret Sauce for Mental Wellness and Well-Being

Ah, self-compassion! It's like a warm, fuzzy blanket for your psyche that's been gaining a lot of buzz lately. What's the big deal? Well, self-compassion is all about treating yourself with kindness, a dash of TLC, and understanding, especially when life throws curveballs or when you feel like you've messed up.

One of the superpowers of self-compassion is silencing that pesky inner critic. You know, the one that loves to remind you of every little mistake and makes you feel like you're the only person in the world who's ever messed up. But guess what? Newsflash: Everyone goofs sometimes! By practicing self-compassion, you can put that inner critic in time-out and start to see your missteps as just part of the human experience.

But wait, there's more! Self-compassion is also like emotional kung-fu, helping you face difficult emotions and experiences with grace and style. When life gets tough, and it feels like everything is falling apart, self-compassion whispers in your ear, "Hey, it's okay. Let's take a deep breath and handle this together." It helps you become a ninja of resilience and fosters a rock-solid sense of self-worth.

As if that's not enough, self-compassion is also a mental health superhero. Studies have shown that those who practice self-compassion are less likely to be weighed down by depression, anxiety, and stress, and they're better equipped to dodge burnout and compassion fatigue. By taking care of Numero Uno (that's you!), you'll have the energy and resources to tackle life's challenges like a boss.

So, in a nutshell, self-compassion is your trusty sidekick for a happier, healthier you. When you treat yourself with kindness, warmth, and understanding, you'll find that negative self-talk takes a back seat, you can power through tough times, and your self-worth and resilience skyrocket. Embrace self-compassion, and you'll be on your way to living your best Secular Buddhist life!

The Self-Compassion Obstacle Course: Recognizing Barriers and Mindfully Smashing Through Them

Oh, self-compassion, you elusive creature! Sometimes, it's like trying to catch a greased pig at the county fair. But never fear, intrepid Secular Buddhists! Let's take a look at some of the barriers that might be holding you back from embracing self-compassion, and let's bust out some mindfulness-based techniques to overcome them.

Barrier 1: The Chatterbox of Doom (aka Negative Self-Talk)

Negative self-talk is like that annoying neighbor who just won't shut up. It can be a massive roadblock to self-compassion. The solution? Transform that chatty Cathy into a cheerleader.

Mindfulness-Based Technique: Mindful Awareness

Channel your inner Sherlock Holmes and start observing your thoughts without judgment. This mindful awareness will help you nip that negative self-talk in the bud and shift to a more positive dialogue.

Barrier 2: The Kryptonite of Compassion (aka Fear of Vulnerability)

Some people are terrified of appearing vulnerable, thinking it's a sign of weakness. This fear can be a major self-compassion buzzkill.

Mindfulness-Based Technique: Self-Compassionate Reflection

Put on your emotional armor and acknowledge your vulnerabilities with kindness and non-judgment. This self-compassionate reflection will help you face your fears and embrace a more compassionate attitude.

Barrier 3: The Perfectionist's Trap

Perfectionism is like a hamster wheel that never stops spinning. If you're always chasing impossible standards, you're setting yourself up for self-criticism and disappointment.

Mindfulness-Based Technique: Mindful Acceptance

Give yourself permission to be imperfect and embrace your limitations. This mindful acceptance will help you break free from the perfectionist's trap and cultivate a more forgiving attitude towards yourself.

Barrier 4: The Art of Ignoring Yourself (aka Lack of Self-Care)

When you're a pro at neglecting your own needs, it's tough to find that self-compassionate sweet spot. But hey, it's time to start treating yourself like the rock star you are!

Mindfulness-Based Technique: Self-Compassionate Action

Roll out the red carpet for self-care and start nurturing your physical and emotional needs with kindness. This self-compassionate action will help you overcome self-neglect and develop a more caring and compassionate relationship with yourself.

In conclusion, identifying these pesky barriers to self-compassion is the first step to overcoming them with some handy-dandy mindfulness-based techniques. By integrating these techniques into your daily life, you'll be well on your way to a kinder, more compassionate you, and an extra helping of happiness and fulfillment. So, let's get cracking on that self-compassion obstacle course and start living our best Secular Buddhist lives!

The Empathy Enigma: How Your Personal Time Machine and Social Playbook Shape Your Ability to Connect

Empathy, that magical ingredient that lets us connect with others like social glue, can be a bit of a mystery. What makes some people more empathetic than others? The answer lies in the twin forces of your personal time machine (aka your past experiences) and your social playbook (aka social conditioning).

Your personal time machine whisks you back to your early years, where your experiences with caregivers shaped your empathy skills. Were you showered with warmth, encouragement, and emotional support? Congrats, you hit the empathy jackpot! But if your childhood was more "emotional desert" than "nurturing oasis," you might find empathy a bit trickier to master.

Now, let's talk about your social playbook. This is where your culture and society come in, whispering in your ear about what's expected, what's valued, and how to treat others. If your social playbook is all about "me, myself, and I," you might struggle to put yourself in someone else's shoes.

When empathy is in short supply, it's like trying to build a Lego castle without any bricks. You'll have a tough time connecting with others and understanding their emotions. This can lead to a serious case of relationship hiccups, both in your personal and professional life.

So, how do you solve the empathy enigma? Start by recognizing the roles your personal time machine and social playbook play in shaping your empathy skills. Reflect on your experiences and cultural conditioning to understand your biases and work on overcoming them. You can also flex your empathy muscles daily by actively listening to others, imagining life in their shoes, or just being a kind and compassionate human being.

With practice and dedication, you'll be well on your way to becoming an empathy rock star, forging deeper connections and living your best Secular Buddhist life!

Mirror, Mirror on the Wall: Using Self-Reflection to Boost Your Compassion and Understanding Superpowers

Empathy, that magical skill that lets us put ourselves in someone else's shoes, can be a bit of a mixed bag. Some people have bucket loads of it, while others are scraping the bottom of the empathy barrel. But don't despair, self-reflection exercises can help you unlock your inner compassion and understanding superhero!

Remember that our past experiences and social conditioning are the dynamic duo that shape our empathy skills. Whether it's childhood memories or cultural influences, these factors can either nurture our empathy or leave it stunted.

So, how do we give our empathy superpowers a boost? It's time to get up close and personal with some self-reflection exercises! Here are some steps to help you view yourself and others with more compassion and understanding:

Step 1: Time-travel through your past

Take a trip down memory lane and examine your past experiences, especially your early years. Reflect on how your upbringing, relationships, and circumstances might have impacted your empathy levels.

Step 2: Decode your social conditioning

Unravel the complex web of social norms, beliefs, and cultural influences that have shaped your understanding of others. Examine any stereotypes, biases, or prejudices you might hold and work on breaking them down.

Step 3: Be your own compassionate coach

Learn to treat yourself with kindness, understanding, and acceptance. When you can view yourself through a compassionate lens, it becomes easier to extend that same compassion to others.

Step 4: Practice, practice, practice

Make empathy a daily habit by actively listening to others, empathizing with their experiences, and offering understanding and support.

By engaging in self-reflection exercises, you can strengthen your empathy superpowers, build deeper connections, and truly embody the principles of Secular Buddhism. So, go on, embrace your inner compassion and understanding superhero, and let's make the world a kinder, more empathetic place!

The Empathy Chronicles: How Understanding Others Supercharges Relationships and Communication Skills

Once upon a time in the land of human interactions, empathy reigned supreme. This magical ability to understand and feel the emotions of others was the secret sauce for building strong relationships and honing communication skills. Let's embark on a journey to explore the marvelous benefits of empathy in our lives!

Benefit 1: Relationship Wizardry

Empathy is the ultimate relationship-building spell. When we show genuine care and understanding, we forge stronger and more fulfilling bonds, whether it's with friends, family, or colleagues. It's the secret to creating relationships that are truly magical.

Benefit 2: Communication Charms

Unleash the power of communication with a touch of empathy! By understanding others' perspectives, we can tailor our messages to resonate with them, preventing misunderstandings and conflicts. In a world filled with miscommunications, empathy is the secret charm that keeps everyone on the same page.

Benefit 3: Teamwork Enchantment

Empathy is the potion that fuels teamwork and collaboration. When we empathize with our fellow adventurers, we create an atmosphere of understanding and appreciation, which can lead to a more harmonious and effective journey towards our common goals.

Benefit 4: Professional Sorcery

In the realm of work, empathy is the key to unlocking employee loyalty and productivity. When employees feel valued and understood, they're more likely to stick around and give their all. Managers, take note: empathy is the magical ingredient for effective leadership!

In conclusion, empathy holds the power to transform our relationships and communication skills, making them positively enchanting. By practicing empathy, we can connect with others on a deeper level, becoming better friends, colleagues, and leaders in the process. So, grab your empathy wand and start generating magic.

The Great Empathy-Sympathy Showdown and the Art of Boundary Setting

Empathy and sympathy might sound like two sides of the same coin, but they're actually more like distant cousins. Empathy is all about putting yourself in someone else's shoes, feeling their emotions alongside them. Sympathy, on the other hand, is like watching from the sidelines, feeling pity or sorrow for another person's struggle.

Understanding the difference between empathy and sympathy is essential for healthy relationships and boundaries. Think of empathy as a comforting hug and sympathy as a pat on the back. A hug offers support and understanding, while a pat on the back is a more detached gesture.

Boundaries, boundaries, boundaries! It's vital to know when to draw the line between empathizing and sympathizing. Constantly taking on someone else's emotions can lead to the dreaded burnout or compassion fatigue, which helps nobody. Empathize, but remember to save some emotional energy for yourself.

So, how do we set those healthy boundaries? First, recognize when you're shouldering someone else's emotions, then take a step back and offer support without playing the hero. It's okay to say, "No, thank you!" to being an emotional dumping ground. Remember, self-care isn't selfish; it's essential.

Clear communication is also key to maintaining healthy boundaries. Let your friends, family, and coworkers know what you can and can't handle. This will help create a more balanced, mutually supportive environment for all involved.

In conclusion, learning to distinguish between empathy and sympathy and setting healthy boundaries leads to a more balanced emotional life. So go ahead, connect deeply with others, but don't forget to save some room for yourself. After all, life's a balancing act!

The Empathy and Compassion Playbook: Five Fun Ways to Connect with Yourself and Others

Compassion and empathy are the power duo you didn't know you needed. They're crucial for building rock-solid relationships, busting stress, and boosting well-being. Ready to level up your empathy game? Here are five fun ways to get started:

1. The Art of Active Listening: This is not just about hearing, but truly understanding what others are saying. Pretend you're a detective, piecing together the clues of their story. Maintain eye contact, nod in agreement, and ask open-ended questions to show you're all ears. Sherlock Holmes, eat your heart out!

2. Gratitude Galore: Time to crank up those warm, fuzzy feelings! Expressing gratitude is like a happiness workout for your brain. List three things you're

grateful for each day or send a heartfelt "thank you" to someone who's made a difference in your life. Watch out, world – you're about to get a whole lot more grateful!

3. Kindness Crusader: It's time to spread kindness like confetti. Perform small acts of kindness for others – hold the door, offer a compliment, or even share a smile. Don't forget to treat yourself too, with a relaxing bath or a leisurely walk. You deserve it, Kindness Crusader!

4. Mindfulness Master: Ready to become a Zen master? Mindfulness is all about being present, aware, and non-judgmental. It's the secret sauce that helps you tune into your emotions and develop empathy. You can practice mindfulness through meditation, deep breathing exercises, or simply soaking in the beauty of your surroundings without distractions. Embrace your inner Buddha and watch your compassion grow.

5. Volunteer Virtuoso: Flex your empathy muscles and make a difference by volunteering. It's a win-win situation - you get to help others and gain insights into their perspectives, while also feeling good about your contributions. Dive into local charity work, join a community service project, or donate to a cause close to your heart. You're now officially a Volunteer Virtuoso!

In conclusion, cultivating compassion and empathy doesn't have to be a chore. With these five fun and practical strategies, you'll strengthen your relationships, improve your well-being, and become an all-around empathy superstar. So go ahead, give these techniques a whirl, and watch as you transform into a more compassionate, empathetic version of yourself.

CHAPTER 5

Taming the Monkey Mind with the Key of Mindfulness

Grasping the Hilarity of Mindfulness and its Significance

Mindfulness, that fine art of being totally present and tuned in to your thoughts, feelings, and surroundings, is a bit like being a detective on the trail of your own emotions. You observe without judgment and accept whatever shenanigans the moment throws at you.

Why is it important, you ask? Well, for starters, it's a fabulous stress-buster and anxiety-reducer, not to mention a champion of focus and concentration. By honing your mindfulness skills, you become your own personal emotion whisperer, leading to more positive and constructive responses. Plus, it's a relationship booster, as you'll be more present and receptive to the needs and feelings of others. Who wouldn't want that?

In this breakneck, information-overloaded world, mindfulness is like a life preserver for your mental health. It helps you hit the brakes, tune in to your needs, and stop reacting like a pinball to every external stimulus. Regular mindfulness practice turns you into a grounded, centered Zen master (well, sort of), ultimately bringing more peace and happiness to your life. No joke!

Mastering the Art of Mindful Living with a Dash of Fun

Practicing mindfulness is like turning your life into a serene oasis amid the whirlwind of work, family, and relationships. It's a great way to manage emotions, reduce stress, and fill your life with more joy and delight.

Here's how to add a pinch of mindfulness magic to your daily grind:

1. Start with your breath, the unsung hero of relaxation

Take a few deep breaths, focusing on the in and out of your body's air supply. Get into the rhythm and let those pesky thoughts sail away like unwanted party guests.

2. Embrace the now, like a zen superhero

Stay present, paying attention to the happenings around you. Resist the urge to time travel into the future with worry or dwell on past shenanigans.

3. Give your senses a workout

Flex your mindfulness muscles by engaging all your senses. Savor the flavors of your food, marvel at nature's colors and textures, and lend your ears to the soundtrack of life.

4. Take mindful timeouts

Hit the pause button throughout the day to get your mindfulness fix. Stroll outside, meditate for a few minutes, or breathe deeply when stress rears its ugly head.

5. Practice gratitude with a smile

Reflect on the good stuff in your life and give thanks for the simple pleasures. Gratitude is a powerful ally in the quest for happiness.

6. Kick distractions to the curb

Take a break from your electronic sidekicks and focus on the here and now. It's amazing how the world comes to life when you're not glued to a screen.

By embracing these tips, you'll infuse your life with mindfulness, boost your presence, and ramp up the calm factor. So go ahead, add a dash of mindfulness to your daily recipe, and savor the increased happiness and contentment.

Tackling Stress and Anxiety with a Hearty Dose of Mindfulness

Mindfulness is like having a personal stress-fighting sidekick, helping you stay aware of your thoughts, feelings, and actions in the present moment. Science backs it up – mindfulness can take a chunk out of stress and anxiety, making our minds and bodies healthier and happier. It's like a superhero cape for our emotional well-being.

To dive into the world of mindfulness, find a quiet spot to park your tush and unwind. Close your eyes, and let your breath take center stage, feeling the air's ebb and flow. If your mind decides to go on an impromptu adventure, kindly escort it back to your breath. You can even sneak mindfulness into everyday activities like walking, cooking, or brushing your teeth. Just zoom in on the task, banish distractions, and soak up the sensory experience.

To boost your stress-busting prowess, make mindfulness a regular part of your routine. Set aside a few minutes each day to give your brain a mindfulness vacation, guided meditations, or a body scan exercise.

Other nifty tricks to kick stress and anxiety to the curb include practicing gratitude, focusing on feel-good affirmations, and releasing negative thoughts and emotions like they're hot potatoes. In the end, mindfulness is a powerful ally in our quest to vanquish stress and anxiety, paving the way for better health and well-being.

Spicing Up Your Daily Life with a Pinch of Mindfulness

Injecting a dose of mindfulness into daily routines and activities is like adding an extra scoop of joy and serenity to your life sundae. Mindfulness is all about being aware of the present moment without passing judgment, letting you live life in full technicolor.

Ready to add some mindful flair to your day-to-day? Try these tips:

Kick-off your day with mindfulness: Begin by taking a few deep breaths and setting a fun intention for the day. Let your breath be the star of the show, and sweep any pesky thoughts off the stage.

Feast on mindful eating: Ditch the habit of wolfing down meals or eating with distractions. Instead, turn mealtime into a sensory smorgasbord, savoring flavors, textures, and aromas like you're a food critic on a mission.

Schedule mindful timeouts: Hit the "pause" button during your day for mini-mindfulness breaks. Close your eyes, breathe deeply, and soak up the present moment. You can even sneak in a meditation session or some yoga to soothe your mind and body.

Embrace gratitude with gusto: Take a few moments daily to count your blessings and appreciate life's gifts, big and small.

Get cozy with nature: Unleash your inner naturalist and bask in the wonders of the great outdoors. Stroll through a park, hike a wooded trail, or simply lounge outside and marvel at the beauty around you.

By weaving mindfulness into your daily life, you'll cultivate a greater sense of calm and contentment, setting the stage for a happier, more satisfying existence. So go ahead, sprinkle some mindfulness magic into your life today, and watch the benefits unfold.

Mindfulness and Self-Compassion: A Dynamic Duo for Personal Growth

They say awareness is the key to personal growth, and that's where mindfulness comes strutting in. Mindfulness is all about fine-tuning our presence in the moment, sans judgment or criticism. It's like turning up the volume on our inner radio, tuning into our thoughts, emotions, and actions with curiosity and openness.

But wait, there's more! To truly rock mindfulness, we need to amp up our self-compassion. Self-compassion is all about treating ourselves with the same TLC we'd give a cherished friend. It means embracing our authentic selves, quirks and all, with patience, understanding, and kindness.

Mindfulness and self-compassion go together like PB&J. Mindfulness helps us become more aware, while self-compassion teaches us to accept ourselves without getting bogged down in self-judgment. This power duo can lead to inner peace, emotional resilience, and mental well-being.

Ready to practice mindfulness and self-compassion? Try these tips:

Pause for a breather: When stress or anxiety strikes, take a moment to tune into your breath. Feel the air flow in and out, and let thoughts and distractions float away. This simple act can anchor you in the present and restore calm.

Celebrate gratitude: Spend a few moments daily savoring life's gifts, from the sun's warm embrace to a loved one's company. Gratitude can help us cultivate self-compassion and savor life's goodness.

Embrace self-forgiveness: We're all human, and we stumble. Instead of raking ourselves over the coals, practice self-forgiveness. By accepting our failures, we can let go and move forward with grace.

Get your mindful groove on: Dive into activities that spark joy and mindfulness, like yoga, meditation, or a nature walk. Focusing on the present moment and immersing ourselves in the activity can nurture self-compassion and contentment.

In a nutshell, mindfulness and self-compassion can unlock the door to inner peace and well-being. By practicing these skills, we can embrace our true selves and foster emotional resilience and contentment.

Mindfulness: Your Secret Weapon for Rocking Relationships and Communication

Did you know mindfulness is like a love potion for your relationships? No kidding! Practicing mindfulness helps us to be fully present and engaged in our interactions, paving the way for more profound connections and mutual understanding.

Ready to infuse mindfulness into your relationships? Start with these tips:

Breathe it in: Focus on your breathing, taking deep, calming breaths. Feel the sensations in your body. Keep this focus as you chat with others, ensuring you stay anchored and present.

Listen like a pro: Be all ears when others speak. Forget about rehearsing your next snappy response; instead, truly grasp their message and empathize with their point of view. This leads to more meaningful, effective communication.

Press pause during conflict: Disagreements happen, but before you leap into battle, take a moment to acknowledge your emotions and reactions. Hitting the pause button can help you respond more thoughtfully and kindly.

In a nutshell, mindfulness is like a secret sauce that can supercharge your relationships and communication skills. By being present and truly "there" in our interactions, we can create deeper connections and understanding with the people we care about. So, give mindfulness a whirl and watch your relationships thrive!

Mindfulness: The Wellness Superpower You Didn't Know You Needed

Get ready to meet your new best friend – regular mindfulness practice! This unsung hero of wellness is here to shower you with benefits for your overall well-being. Let's check out what it has to offer:

Stress and anxiety? Say goodbye: Mindfulness meditation helps you get acquainted with your thoughts and emotions, teaching you to release negativity and focus on the present. The result? Less stress and anxiety.

Level-up mental clarity and focus: With mindfulness, you can boost your mental prowess, making you a productivity and efficiency machine in daily tasks.

Invincible immunity: Mindfulness can give your immune system a helping hand, meaning fewer sick days and better overall health.

Hello, self-awareness: Get ready for increased confidence and better decision-making, courtesy of a healthy dose of self-awareness that mindfulness brings.

Emotions? No problem: Mindfulness helps you accept and understand your emotions without judgment, leading to increased emotional intelligence and stability.

Life satisfaction: Mindfulness sprinkles happiness, contentment, and improved quality of life all over your day-to-day experience.

But wait, there's more! Regular mindfulness practice can also amp up your empathy, deepen connections with others, and help you become more resilient and adaptable in the face of life's curveballs. So, what are you waiting for? Embrace mindfulness and let the wellness revolution begin!

CHAPTER 6

Slowing Down to Smell the Roses: Exploring Meditation Techniques for Cultivating Inner Peace

A Crash Course in Meditation: Finding Inner Zen with a Dash of Laughter

Mindfulness meditation, the art of chilling out and tuning into your thoughts, feelings, and bodily sensations, is like a mental spa day. And who doesn't love a good spa day? Turns out, this simple yet oh-so-satisfying mental practice can have some pretty impressive benefits when you make it a habit.

First up, say goodbye to stress and anxiety! With regular mindfulness meditation, you become a master of your emotions, like a superhero of the mind. You'll gain better control over those pesky feelings and lower the chances of stress-related party crashers like depression, insomnia, and chronic pain.

Next, get ready to paint your world with positivity! Mindfulness is like a magic wand that helps you transform negative thoughts into beautiful rainbows. Learn to dodge those triggers that bring you down and focus on the good stuff instead. Voila! You're the proud owner of a brighter outlook on life.

Third, mindfulness sharpens your decision-making prowess. Being more in tune with your inner world helps you think clearer and more objectively. The result? You'll make better choices that align with your values and goals – like a true-life Jedi.

Finally, mindfulness unleashes your inner empath. As you become more aware of your own thoughts and emotions, you start to really "get" what others are going through, too. This newfound empathy and compassion make your relationships healthier and more satisfying, like a warm hug for the soul.

In a nutshell, mindfulness practice turns you into a calmer, less stressed, and emotionally balanced superstar. You'll be more productive and make smarter decisions. Over time, your life will feel like a five-star resort, all thanks to the power of mindfulness meditation.

Mindfulness Meditation: Becoming a Self-Awareness Ninja in the Now

First things first: scout out a quiet, comfy spot where no one will disturb your zen moment. Once you're settled in your meditation fortress, take a few deep breaths and let relaxation wash over you like a warm bath.

Now, focus on the present moment like you're Sherlock Holmes on the case. Notice the sensations in your body, thoughts, emotions, sounds, and smells around you. The key here is to be a curious observer without any judgment or the urge to play Mother Nature.

As you dive deeper into your present experience, let your curiosity lead the way. Explore the feeling of being entirely in the now without needing to slap labels on anything.

When thoughts or emotions pop up like unexpected party guests, greet them with a nod but don't cling to them. Let them come and go without judging them or sending out a search party if they leave.

If your mind starts to wander like an adventurous puppy, gently guide it back to your body and breath. Remember, mindfulness meditation is a practice, and it's okay if your mind occasionally goes on a little detour.

As you get the hang of mindfulness meditation, you'll start to see your thoughts and emotions more clearly, like a mind-reading superhero. This heightened self-awareness can help you embrace yourself and your present experience without judgment.

Soak up this awareness and acceptance for a few more minutes, appreciating the chance to infuse mindfulness into your daily life. When you're ready, ease your attention back to your surroundings and open your eyes, ready to face the world as a self-awareness ninja.

Loving-Kindness Meditation: Channel Your Inner Love Guru for Yourself and Others

Find a comfy seat, sit up straight like royalty, and plant those feet firmly on the ground. Close your eyes, take a few breaths that would make Darth Vader proud, and let's get this love train started.

First, think of someone who's been a thorn in your side. Picture their face, and imagine them standing right in front of you. See them as just another flawed human, like the rest of us mere mortals.

Whisper these sweet nothings to yourself:

"May you be happy.

May you be healthy.

May you be safe.

May you live with ease."

As you recite these words, picture yourself sending them a giant, warm-hearted hug of forgiveness. Let go of the grudges, resentment, or hurt feelings, and fill your heart with love and compassion instead.

Next, think of a time when you played the role of the pesky thorn. Remember, you're also a perfectly imperfect human. Repeat these phrases, now directed at yourself:

"May I be happy.

May I be healthy.

May I be safe.

May I live with ease."

As you say these words, imagine showering yourself with compassion and forgiveness. Say "bye-bye" to guilt and shame, and welcome in love and acceptance.

Finally, picture everyone you've ever known (yes, even that kid who stole your lunch money in third grade). Whisper these universal well-wishes:

"May all beings be happy.

May all beings be healthy.

May all beings be safe.

May all beings live with ease."

Picture yourself as a love-spreading superhero, sending out waves of compassion to every living being. Bask in this loving energy for a bit, then take a few deep breaths and open your eyes, ready to sprinkle love and kindness throughout your day.

Breathing Techniques: The Stress-Busting, Anxiety-Crushing Guide to Ultimate Relaxation

For centuries, humans have been using breathing techniques to calm their minds and kick stress and anxiety to the curb. If you're looking to wrestle your emotions into submission, try these relaxation-inducing breathing techniques:

1. Deep Breathing: Find a quiet, comfy spot to sit or lie down. Inhale deeply through your nose, then hold your breath like you're going for the world record. Slowly exhale through your mouth and repeat, focusing on your breath and imagining your tension evaporating like morning dew.

2. Counted Breathing: Inhale through your nose and count to four, like you're counting sheep. Hold your breath for four counts, then exhale through your

mouth, counting to four again. Repeat, letting the counting clear your mind and lull your body into relaxation mode.

3. Equal Breathing: Inhale deeply through your nose, counting to four. Then, exhale slowly through your mouth, counting to four again. Keep your inhales and exhales equal in length, like you're measuring the perfect recipe for relaxation.

4. Belly Breathing: Put one hand on your belly and the other on your chest. Inhale deeply, feeling your belly rise like a well-proofed loaf of bread while your chest stays put. Exhale slowly through your mouth, feeling your belly deflate. Focus on the sensation of your breath dancing through your body.

5. Alternate Nostril Breathing: Plug one nostril with your finger and inhale deeply through the other, like you're sniffing out a mystery. Hold your breath for a few seconds, then close the other nostril and exhale through the first. Keep alternating nostrils for a one-of-a-kind relaxation experience.

Breathing techniques are like portable stress-relief ninjas – they can be practiced anytime, anywhere. Incorporate these techniques into your daily routine and watch your mental health and overall well-being soar.

Lights, Camera, Visualization: Unleashing Your Creative Superpowers, Healing Energy, and Manifestation Mojo

Close your eyes and take a deep breath in, letting your worries and thoughts dissolve like cotton candy in water. Keep breathing deeply, sinking into a state of relaxation so peaceful, you could snooze on a bed of marshmallows.

Picture yourself lounging in a gorgeous open field. You're surrounded by technicolor flowers, the grass sways like it's dancing to a slow jam, and the sun is cuddling your skin with its warmth.

Imagine a small, glowing disco ball of light in the center of your chest. This funky light represents your creative genius, your manifestation muscle, and your healing vibes. Feel it pulsating with energy, ready to party.

Now, let your mind wander to your desired outcome. Whatever it is you want to create or manifest, visualize it in 4K resolution. It's as real as your favorite pizza joint – already there, just waiting for you to enjoy it.

Merge your intention with your chest's disco ball of light. Feel it expand like the ultimate light show, filling your body and beyond. This energy radiates outwards, turning the field into a dazzling display of brilliance.

Keep focusing on your intention and glowing light show, feeling the energy surging through and around you. You're plugged into the universe's power outlet, harnessing its infinite energy.

Take a few more deep breaths and, when you're ready, start reconnecting with your physical body. Wiggle your extremities like you're waking up from the world's best nap. Take one more satisfying breath in, and open your eyes.

Use this visualization meditation whenever you want to turbocharge your creativity, healing, or manifestation game. Just imagine that groovy disco ball of light and your desired outcome, and let the energy flow. Before you know it, you'll be a manifestation master, wielding your creative powers like a superhero.

Mantra Madness: Channel Your Inner Superstar, Summon Good Vibes, and High-Five the Divine

Get comfy in your favorite sitting position, close your eyes, and take a deep breath. As you exhale, imagine your tension and worry being carried away by a team of tiny stress-relief fairies.

Whisper this mantra to yourself like it's a top-secret code: "I am a divine being, filled with love and light."

Picture a radiant, toasty light engulfing you, filling every nook and cranny of your being – from your noggin to your tootsies. Let this light gift you with peace, clarity, and joy that makes you want to do a happy dance.

Keep repeating the mantra while focusing on your breath, letting distracting thoughts float by like clouds in a sky of zen. Nod at them, but don't invite them to your peace party.

Soak up the good vibes and emotions as you high-five the divine. Wrap yourself in a cozy blanket of love and light.

When you're ready, gently open your eyes, inhale one last invigorating breath, and strut into your day, feeling connected to the universe and ready to rock 'n' roll.

Tips to Rock Your Meditation Game: Small Steps, Realistic Goals, and Nailing Distractions with Mindfulness

Start small, like a tiny meditation ninja: Kick off with short meditation sessions, just 5-10 minutes each day. No need to aim for marathon sittings right away.

Set goals you can actually achieve: Keep it real, like meditating for 5 minutes a day, every day. You'll feel like a meditation superhero!

Find your meditation lair: Choose a quiet, comfy spot to help you focus and dodge distractions. Sitting in the same spot every time creates a sense of "Oh yeah, it's meditation time!"

Rock out with guided meditation: Get your groove on with guided meditations. Apps aplenty offer these gems to help you start your meditation party.

Weave meditation into your daily routine: Make meditation a part of your daily life – schedule it for mornings, evenings, or whenever you need a relaxation recharge.

Tackle distractions with mindfulness: Observe and high-five those distractions, then gently guide your mind back to your practice like a meditation bouncer.

Practice like a boss: Consistency is the key to becoming a meditation rock star. Commit to your meditation jam sessions and stick to it.

Patience, grasshopper: Remember, meditation is a practice, and it takes time to master. If your mind wanders or you miss a session, don't sweat it. You're still awesome!

By following these tips, you'll establish a regular meditation practice and make it a part of your daily life, slaying distractions and hurdles like a meditation superhero.

CHAPTER 7

Battling Your Inner Demons: Confronting Negative Emotions and Thoughts

The Surprising Perks of Negativity: Embracing Our Inner Grump

Picture yourself as a human with a rollercoaster of emotions – a colorful blend of joy, sadness, and everything in between. In the wild realm of Secular Buddhism, we say "embrace the grump" because, believe it or not, those pesky negative emotions and thoughts do have a role in our daily lives.

Feeling blue? Angry? Anxious? No worries, you're not alone. These emotions are like your own personal life coach, pushing you to fix what's bothering you. Anxiety about an exam? You'll likely find yourself hitting the books like a caffeine-fueled student. Sad about a loss? It's nature's way of helping you process that sorrow and ultimately cherish the memories you've made.

And what about those pesky negative thoughts? They're not just uninvited party-crashers, but little nudges pointing you towards areas for improvement. Constant self-criticism? Time to amp up the self-love and give yourself a hefty dose of compassion.

But beware, dear reader! There's a fine line between functional negativity and the overwhelming kind. If you find yourself drowning in a sea of pessimism, don't hesitate to throw yourself a lifeline by seeking help from a therapist or counselor.

So, fellow travelers on this rollercoaster called life, let's give a shout-out to our inner grump. By understanding and taming our negative emotions and thoughts, we can harness their power for personal growth and improved well-being. Remember, in the world of Secular Buddhism, it's all about balance.

The Usual Suspects: Unmasking the Culprits Behind Negativity

Let's face it, life can sometimes feel like a parade of gloomy thoughts and emotions. But don't let that get you down! In the adventurous world of Secular

Buddhism, we're all about identifying the usual suspects behind our negative emotions and thoughts, so we can manage them like pros.

Stress: This sneaky little rascal loves to ambush us with anxiety, depression, and frustration. Watch your back, stress!

Trauma: A blast from the past can be more than just a bad hair day. Trauma can bring fear, anxiety, and flashbacks to the party.

Relationship drama: When the love boat hits rocky waters, negativity can set sail with feelings like anger, jealousy, and resentment.

Money matters: When our piggy bank feels light, stress, anxiety, and frustration can weigh heavy on our minds.

Health hiccups: Feeling under the weather? Depression, sadness, and anxiety might come knocking, both physically and mentally.

Self-doubt: That little voice in your head spewing self-doubt can unleash a torrent of fear, anxiety, and depression.

Social media: Scrolling through picture-perfect lives can trigger envy, jealousy, and self-esteem nosedives. Keep it real, folks!

Sleepless nights: Burning the midnight oil can leave us with irritability, mood swings, and depression.

So, what's the game plan? Recognize these triggers and tackle them head-on! From stress management techniques and therapy to better communication, smarter finances, and a good night's sleep, managing these triggers can help us kick negativity to the curb and improve our mental health and overall well-being.

Becoming a Mindfulness Ninja: Tackling Negativity with Self-Awareness

Ready to level up your emotional Kung Fu? Embrace your inner mindfulness ninja and take charge of those negative emotions and thoughts! By cultivating self-awareness and mindfulness, we can transform ourselves into emotional warriors, ready to tackle whatever life throws our way.

First stop: mindfulness meditation. Close your eyes, breathe, and let the present moment envelop you like a warm hug. As you become one with the here and now, you'll find yourself more in tune with your emotions and better equipped to detect those pesky triggers that set off negativity.

Want more self-awareness superpowers? Engage in self-reflection by journaling or confiding in a trusted friend or therapist. You'll soon understand your emotional landscape like a seasoned cartographer, mapping out the best routes to navigate life's challenges.

With your newfound self-awareness, it's time to unleash some powerful techniques to manage negativity. Reframe those nagging thoughts with positive self-talk or summon relaxation techniques like deep breathing or progressive muscle relaxation to calm your mind and body.

Remember, becoming a mindfulness ninja is a lifelong quest, but the journey is filled with the rewards of greater compassion, intention, and authenticity. So, grab your emotional nunchucks and let's conquer negativity together!

Becoming a Positivity Wizard: Conquering Negative Thoughts with Good Vibes

Ready to wave your magic wand and banish those pesky negative thoughts? Transform yourself into a Positivity Wizard with these enchanting tips to shift your mindset and boost your mental health. With these powerful spells, you'll be brewing up optimism and resilience in no time!

Cast a Mindfulness Spell: Be present and accept your thoughts and feelings without judgment. By observing your negative thoughts from a distance, you'll learn they don't define you.

Unmask Negative Self-Talk: Keep a journal to reveal the sneaky situations that trigger negative thoughts. This knowledge will empower you to conjure up strategies for countering the darkness.

Duel with Negative Thoughts: Challenge your inner naysayer with evidence-based, alternative thoughts. Counter "I'm not good enough" with "I've achieved so much and will continue to grow."

Summon Gratitude: Start each day with a gratitude ritual and keep a blessings journal to shift your focus from gloom to glee.

Craft Affirmations: Concoct powerful, positive affirmations and chant them like a mantra to rewire your brain for sunnier thinking.

Seek Positive Company: Surround yourself with people who cast a warm, uplifting glow on your life. Steer clear of those who trigger negativity.

Call for Reinforcements: If negative thoughts persist, enlist the help of a therapist or counselor. They can teach you advanced spells for managing negative thought patterns and boosting well-being.

By practicing the art of positivity and cognitive strategies, you'll create a reality filled with good vibes and improved mental health. Embrace your inner Positivity Wizard and let the magic flow!

Assembling Your Emotional Avengers: Building a Support Network and Calling in the Experts

Gather your Emotional Avengers and save the day when it comes to your mental health! Assemble a team of supportive, empathetic individuals who offer a listening ear, encouragement, and a hearty high-five when you need it most.

Your support network can include family and friends, who are the trusty sidekicks in your emotional superhero squad. They're there to lend a helping hand or crack a joke when the going gets tough.

Don't forget to seek out support groups, where you'll meet fellow superheroes facing similar challenges. These groups provide a safe space for sharing experiences, swapping tips, and forming a team to tackle life's obstacles.

But sometimes, even superheroes need to call in the experts. When the going gets really tough, it's time to seek professional help from therapists or psychiatrists. They're the elite members of your Emotional Avengers, armed with the knowledge and skills to help you face mental health villains head-on.

There's a whole arsenal of resources available, including face-to-face therapy, online therapy, and teletherapy. These options provide a confidential space to discuss your battles and equip you with an array of mental health weaponry, like cognitive-behavioral therapy, medication management, and mindfulness-based stress reduction.

So, round up your Emotional Avengers and prioritize mental health together. Whether it's leaning on your support network or calling in the experts, every superhero needs a team to save the day. Let's unite and conquer mental health challenges with the power of friendship and professional help!

Stress-Busting Superpowers: Unleashing Exercise, Meditation, and Deep Breathing

Stress lurks around every corner of our modern lives, waiting to pounce like a mischievous gremlin. But fear not, for you possess stress-busting superpowers! By embracing exercise, meditation, and deep breathing, you can vanquish stress and embrace a healthier, more joyful existence.

Unleash your Exercise Powers: Transform into a stress-fighting superhero by flexing your exercise muscles. Endorphins will flood your body, creating a surge of relaxation and happiness. Even a brisk walk or a mini stretching session can send stress scurrying away.

Summon the Magic of Meditation: Conjure up an oasis of calm amidst life's chaos with meditation. Harness the power of mindfulness and deep relaxation, leaving stress quivering in your wake. As you focus on your breath or a mantra, you'll find yourself transported to a serene sanctuary.

Breathe Your Way to Tranquility: With the art of deep breathing, like diaphragmatic breathing, you'll wield a calming force that dissolves stress. Take slow, belly-expanding breaths to restore balance and harmony to your body and mind.

All these stress-busting superpowers can be honed through practice and integrated into your daily life. As you cultivate these skills, you'll enjoy the lasting benefits of reduced stress and a more vibrant, healthy life. Now go forth and conquer stress with your newfound superpowers!

The Self-Care Fiesta: Dancing with Positivity and Self-Compassion

Self-care is like throwing a fiesta for your mental and physical well-being. In the midst of life's hustle, it's easy to forget that we deserve to party with positivity and self-compassion. So, let's crank up the self-care tunes and dance our way to a healthier, happier life.

Join the Positivity Conga Line: Shake off negativity by embracing an upbeat attitude. Focus on the good, practice gratitude, and reframe gloomy thoughts. Surround yourself with people who bring sunshine to your life, and watch your resilience soar.

Salsa with Self-Compassion: Treat yourself like your own best friend, dishing out kindness, understanding, and generous doses of TLC. Embrace your unique blend of strengths and quirks, and give yourself permission to rest, say "no," and prioritize your well-being.

Dance the Self-Care Cha-Cha: Self-care doesn't have to break the bank or take up hours of your day. It can be as simple as a nature walk, jamming to your favorite tunes, or indulging in a few soul-soothing breaths. Establish a self-care routine that keeps you grooving to the beat of well-being.

In a nutshell, the self-care fiesta is all about letting positivity and self-compassion take center stage. By nourishing your mind, body, and soul, you'll not only survive life's challenges but also savor its joys. So go ahead, shake your self-care maracas and let the fiesta begin!

CHAPTER 8

Letting Go of the Monkey Mind: Embracing Impermanence and Non-Attachment

Embracing Life's Ephemeral Nature: Impermanence, Non-Attachment, and Finding Inner Chillness

Life is like a rollercoaster: one minute, you're holding on tight to your favorite stuffed animal (admit it, we all have one), the next minute, you're trying to cope with the horrifying reality of adulthood—taxes, anyone? In this wild ride we call life, it's important to understand that everything around us is temporary and ever-changing. Meet impermanence, the not-so-secret truth that teaches us how to ride life's waves with grace and style.

If you want to find your zen and inner peace, it's time to embrace impermanence like a long-lost friend. By realizing that everything is fleeting, we can let go of unhealthy attachments and see the world as it is: a kaleidoscope of experiences that don't last forever (kind of like that mullet haircut you rocked in the '90s).

Non-attachment is the trendy cousin of impermanence, teaching us how to loosen our grip on things, people, and situations. With non-attachment as our guide, we learn to appreciate life's moments without desperately clinging to them like a koala to a tree. This mindset helps us become cooler cucumbers when faced with change, finding inner peace in our ever-evolving world.

By practicing non-attachment, we stop obsessing over the past and future, and start living in the present, savoring each moment like a scoop of mint chocolate chip ice cream on a hot summer day. We let go of anxiety and worry, trading them in for joy, gratitude, and some much-needed tranquility.

So there you have it, folks! Embrace impermanence and non-attachment, and you'll be well on your way to finding true inner peace and contentment. After all, who wouldn't want to live a worry-free life filled with gratitude and serenity? Trust me, it's a game-changer.

Riding Life's Whirlwind: Impermanence, the Ultimate Bittersweet Symphony

Let's face it, folks: life is like a box of chocolates—you never know what you're going to get, and eventually, it's going to melt. Welcome to the rollercoaster that is impermanence, where everything's changing, and nothing sticks around forever (including those pesky chocolate stains).

Impermanence can feel like a double-edged sword. On one side, it's a bit of a downer to think that all the things we love—our favorite coffee mug, our lucky socks, even our BFFs—are just temporary guests in our lives. It's like a cosmic reminder that we should never get too attached to anything (except maybe our favorite brand of toilet paper).

But on the bright side, impermanence is actually pretty liberating! It's like a get-out-of-jail-free card for life's worries and anxieties. When we accept that everything's always changing, we can stop stressing about things we can't control and start enjoying the present moment (hello, dance party in the living room!).

Embracing impermanence makes us more like life's surfers, able to ride the waves of change with grace and a sense of humor. We become experts at appreciating the fleeting beauty of each moment and the unique tapestry of experiences that make up our lives.

So, let's celebrate the bittersweet symphony of impermanence! By understanding that everything is interconnected and constantly changing, we can appreciate the bigger picture and make a positive impact in our oh-so-brief time on this spinning rock we call Earth. Carpe diem, my friends!

Non-Attachment: The Art of Letting Go and Embracing Inner Joy (No Bungee Cords Required)

Picture this: you're holding onto your favorite coffee mug like it's the Holy Grail. Suddenly, the mug slips from your grasp, and you're left clutching air. Enter non-attachment, the mental karate that teaches us how to let go and find happiness within ourselves, rather than relying on our treasured coffee mugs (or people, or experiences).

Non-attachment, a cornerstone of many Eastern philosophies, reminds us that everything in life is as fleeting as a Snapchat message, so it's pointless to get too attached. Instead of desperately clinging to our prized possessions, relationships, or experiences like a sailor to a life raft, non-attachment encourages us to loosen our grip and accept that nothing lasts forever (except maybe fruitcake).

By practicing non-attachment, we're not turning into emotionless robots. Quite the contrary! We're learning to appreciate life's ebb and flow without drowning in the emotional turmoil that comes with attachment. We become the eye of the storm, calm and composed amidst life's uncertainties.

Non-attachment is like a mental fanny pack (hear me out): it helps us travel through life with a sense of ease and contentment, keeping our hands free to enjoy the journey. So, let's practice the art of letting go and embrace the fleeting beauty of life, knowing that the only constant is change. And remember, no bungee cords required!

Impermanence and Non-Attachment: Unlocking the Secret to a Worry-Free Life (No Time Machine Needed)

Picture this: you're clutching your favorite umbrella, waiting for the storm to pass, but the wind is relentless, and you're left soaking wet. Life can feel like a never-ending storm sometimes, but by embracing impermanence and non-attachment, we can become storm chasers, dancing in the rain with carefree abandon.

We've all been conditioned to cling to things, people, and experiences like they're our last slice of pizza. But holding on too tightly just sets us up for a world of disappointment, anxiety, and a severe case of FOMO (Fear of Missing Out).

When we realize that everything is as transient as a bubble in the wind, we can start to let go of our need for control and accept life's twists and turns. This frees us from the shackles of fear, anxiety, and disappointment, allowing us to kick back, relax, and live in the present moment like a zen master.

Living in the now is like having a front-row seat at the greatest show on Earth. We can savor life's fleeting moments, find joy in the little things, and cherish our relationships without the emotional baggage that comes with attachment.

Non-attachment is like a trusty umbrella (minus the wind), helping us navigate life's storms with a sense of ease and grace. It enables us to overcome our fears of the unknown and uncontrollable, opening the door to new experiences, personal growth, and a whole lot of fun.

So, let's embark on the journey of embracing impermanence and non-attachment, and discover the secret to a worry-free life. Who needs a time machine when we can live fully in the present moment and make the most of every experience? Carpe diem, my friends!

Non-Attachment: The Recipe for a Fulfilled Life (No Superpowers Required)

Picture yourself trying to control every aspect of a surprise party (hint: it's not going to work). In a similar vein, cultivating non-attachment is about letting go of control and embracing life's uncertainties like a roller coaster enthusiast.

Non-attachment is like the secret sauce to living a more fulfilled life, and it's cooked up with a healthy serving of acceptance, a dash of mindfulness, and a willingness to surrender control. Sounds simple, right? Well, it can be challenging, but oh-so-rewarding!

First up, acceptance: the magical ingredient that helps us acknowledge the reality of our situation, rather than wishing we were in a parallel universe. Acceptance teaches us to let go of our need to micromanage and embrace life's surprises with open arms.

Next, we have mindfulness: the art of being fully present and in tune with our thoughts and emotions, without getting caught up in a mental tornado. Mindfulness is like our internal GPS, guiding us through life's twists and turns without getting lost in our attachments and desires.

Finally, the pièce de résistance: letting go of control. This can be as tough as trying to control a room full of puppies, but it's essential for cultivating non-attachment. Surrendering control means trusting in life's journey and being open to the unknown, like a brave explorer setting sail into uncharted waters.

The result? A delicious concoction of peace, contentment, and a deeper understanding of life's impermanence. By cultivating non-attachment, we can savor the present moment and live a more joyful, fulfilling life - no superpowers required! So, let's get cooking and embrace the recipe for a more fulfilled life. Bon appétit!

Impermanence & Non-Attachment: Your Secret Pass to Compassion, Empathy, and Gratitude

Picture this: you're watching a spectacular fireworks display, and you know that each burst of color will soon vanish into the night sky. It's this very impermanence that makes the show so awe-inspiring. Similarly, accepting life's fleeting nature can lead us to embrace impermanence and non-attachment, opening the door to deeper compassion, empathy, and gratitude.

It's like trading in your emotional baggage for a VIP pass to a more mindful and fulfilling life. Letting go of expectations and attachments helps us tune into the present moment and appreciate life's precious, ephemeral experiences.

By practicing non-attachment, we can also level-up our compassion and empathy game. When we're not fixated on our own desires and expectations, we're more open to understanding other people's perspectives and experiences, like a true empathy ninja.

And don't forget about gratitude! Embracing impermanence is like putting on a pair of gratitude goggles, allowing us to see the beauty in the simple things, such as a breathtaking sunset, a scrumptious meal, or a heartwarming hug.

In a nutshell, impermanence and non-attachment are like keys that unlock a treasure chest of compassion, empathy, and gratitude. So, what are you waiting for? Grab those keys and start embracing life's fleeting moments, deepening your connections with others, and feeling grateful for all the world has to offer.

Life's Roller Coaster: How Impermanence and Non-Attachment Are Your Tickets to Strength, Resilience, and Inner Peace

Life is like a roller coaster ride - it's full of unexpected twists, turns, and stomach-churning drops. And just like on a roller coaster, we often cling to anything we can find to give us a sense of stability and security.

But here's the catch: everything in life is impermanent, so holding on for dear life won't save us from change. Instead, we need to embrace the wild ride and learn to let go by practicing impermanence and non-attachment.

Impermanence is like the superhero of change, reminding us that everything in life is temporary and subject to transformation. When we embrace impermanence, we become more flexible and adaptable, ready to take on whatever life throws our way.

Non-attachment, on the other hand, is like our emotional bodyguard, protecting us from depending too much on external things for happiness. It teaches us to detach from our desires and expectations, and to find inner peace regardless of what's happening around us.

By practicing impermanence and non-attachment, we can face life's ups and downs with strength, resilience, and inner peace. We learn to accept change, let go of our worries and anxieties, and appreciate the present moment for what it is.

So, buckle up and get ready to embrace the roller coaster of life with open arms. With impermanence and non-attachment by your side, you'll be better equipped to navigate life's twists and turns, making your journey more fulfilling and meaningful. And who knows? You might even start to enjoy the ride!

CHAPTER 9

. Finding Yourself in the Here and Now: Uncovering Meaning in Life through Secular Buddhism

Delving into the Hilarious World of Secular Buddhism: Finding Life's Meaning sans the Supernatural and Stuffy Doctrines

Welcome to Secular Buddhism, where you can explore the wisdom of Buddha without the supernatural mumbo jumbo and stuffy religious doctrines. Picture it: a Buddhism that's all about getting your Zen on, minus the karma, rebirth, and deities.

So, what's the deal with secular Buddhism? It's all about living in the moment, practicing mindfulness, and being kind to yourself and others. In short, it's about making life a barrel of laughs while staying grounded in reality.

First up, let's chat about impermanence, the idea that everything is as fleeting as a Snapchat story. By understanding that nothing lasts forever (except maybe the embarrassing photos from your last office party), we learn to let go of attachments and desires that can make us suffer. Embrace the present, forget the past, and don't stress about the future – just enjoy the ride!

Next, we have mindfulness: the art of being present and observing your thoughts, feelings, and sensations like a detective on a stakeout, without any judgment. Mindfulness helps you crack the case of your mind's inner workings, identifying the patterns that lead to suffering and cultivating more positive mental states, such as compassion and gratitude. Think of it as your personal happiness magnifying glass.

But wait, there's more! Secular Buddhism also highlights ethical conduct through the Eightfold Path, a spiritual GPS that keeps you on track. This includes actions like dodging harmful behavior, speaking the truth, and showering kindness and generosity on others like confetti at a parade. By sticking to these principles, you'll create a fulfilling, meaningful life without needing an external rule book or celestial approval.

So, there you have it: Secular Buddhism, a practical and down-to-earth approach to life that doesn't rely on supernatural beliefs or traditional religious doctrines. Embrace impermanence, practice mindfulness, and follow the Eightfold Path, and you'll cultivate a sense of purpose and meaning that's grounded in your own experiences and observations. It's like a spiritual sitcom, and you're the star!

Dukkha: The Unbearable Lightness of Suffering and How to Tackle It with Secular Buddhist Practices Like Mindfulness Meditation and Compassion in Action

Ah, dukkha - the Buddhist concept of suffering that's as tricky to escape as a never-ending group text. You know the feeling: life's unsatisfactory nature, the existential FOMO, and the nagging suspicion that there's something more. Dukkha springs from the impermanence of our existence and our clinginess to fleeting things, but our thoughts and perceptions can also turn life's rollercoaster ride into a vicious cycle of negativity.

Enter secular Buddhism, armed with mindfulness meditation, the Swiss Army knife of mental wellness tools. Mindfulness is all about being a present-focused ninja, observing your thoughts, feelings, and bodily sensations like a mental Sherlock Holmes. With practice, you can let go of those pesky thought patterns that lead to suffering, making room for more joy and serenity.

But wait! Secular Buddhism has another ace up its sleeve: compassionate action. This is like the superhero version of kindness, where you swoop in to alleviate the suffering of others through acts of compassion and generosity. By recognizing that we're all in this together, interconnected like an intricate spiderweb, we can find meaning and purpose while making the world a better place.

So, with mindfulness and compassionate action, dukkha doesn't stand a chance. As a secular Buddhist, you'll become an emotional ninja, tackling the roots of suffering and spreading good vibes like a happiness contagion. Together, we can build a world where suffering is reduced, and peace and compassion reign supreme. And who wouldn't want to live in a world like that?

The Four Noble Truths and the Noble Eightfold Path: A Laugh-Out-Loud Guide to Finding Enlightenment and Secular Awesomeness

Picture the Four Noble Truths and the Noble Eightfold Path as Buddhism's "greatest hits" – the timeless principles that guide us toward wisdom, ethics, and mental discipline. And guess what? They're not just for the spiritually devout; these principles can be adapted for secular use, turning them into a one-size-fits-all self-improvement plan.

First, let's get to know the Four Noble Truths: 1) Life comes with a side of suffering, 2) Suffering springs from craving and attachment, 3) You can kick suffering to the curb, and 4) The way to do it is by following the Noble Eightfold Path. The Noble Eightfold Path is like a spiritual checklist that guides you toward enlightenment: right understanding, right intention, right speech, right action, right livelihood, right effort, right mindfulness, and right concentration.

Think of the first two Noble Truths as the "why" of suffering. By understanding suffering and its causes, we can learn to face life's challenges with the grace of a swan. Recognizing that craving and attachment fuel our suffering helps us work on letting go like an emotional Marie Kondo.

Now, let's talk about the Noble Eightfold Path, which is all about living your best life while honing wisdom, ethics, and mental discipline. Start with right understanding and right intention to set a solid foundation. Move on to right speech, right action, and right livelihood to live in harmony with your values and cultivate positive relationships. Finally, practice right effort, right mindfulness, and right concentration to achieve mental mastery and a deeper understanding of yourself and the world.

But can these principles really work for secular folks? You bet! Strip away the religious trappings of Buddhism, and you're left with a versatile guide for developing a meaningful life. Focus on ethical values, personal growth, and compassion for others, and you'll create a path that helps you live a fulfilling life in tune with yourself and the world.

In a nutshell, the Four Noble Truths and the Noble Eightfold Path are your roadmap to wisdom, ethics, and mental discipline. Whether you're a devout Buddhist or a secular seeker, understanding and practicing these principles can help you rise above suffering and live a life that's as rich and fulfilling as a triple chocolate cake. So go ahead, dig in, and savor every bite of this delicious journey!

The Power of Community and Connection in Secular Buddhism: How Your Spiritual Squad Can Supercharge Your Journey to Meaning and Purpose

Picture secular Buddhism as a solo road trip through the landscape of self-discovery, where you're the driver, navigator, and DJ all rolled into one. While this introspective journey can be rewarding, it's no secret that having some travel buddies can make the ride a whole lot more enjoyable. Enter the power of community and connection: your spiritual GPS guiding you to meaning and purpose.

There's no denying that community and connection are the secret sauce in secular Buddhism. Practicing mindfulness and introspection can sometimes feel lonely, like being the only one at a party who doesn't know the dance moves. But when you're part of a tribe of like-minded individuals, you'll find that sense of belonging and shared purpose that makes everything click.

A supportive network isn't just a feel-good bonus; it can also keep you on track when life throws you a curveball. Just like a workout buddy, your spiritual squad will motivate and encourage you to stick with your practice, even when the going gets tough.

But wait, there's more! Community and connection can expand your horizons, introducing you to fresh perspectives and understandings of the teachings. Imagine a melting pot of ideas, where people from diverse backgrounds come together to share their wisdom - it's like a spiritual buffet offering endless food for thought.

The benefits don't stop there. In a supportive community, you'll find a treasure trove of knowledge and skills, with everyone bringing their unique talents to the table. It's like a spiritual skills exchange, where you can learn and grow while helping others do the same.

Lastly, having a supportive network means you don't have to face life's challenges alone. When the going gets tough, your spiritual squad has your back, offering the encouragement and support you need to tackle obstacles head-on and continue your journey.

In a nutshell, community and connection are the unsung heroes of secular Buddhism. They provide the camaraderie, motivation, and support you need to embark on your quest for meaning and purpose. So gather your spiritual squad, and together, you'll conquer the road ahead, transforming self-discovery into a group adventure you'll never forget.

When Secular Buddhism Met Other Philosophies: A Philosophical Love Story of Intersection and Divergence

Picture secular Buddhism as a spiritual and philosophical superhero, flying into the fray to make sense of life's big questions. It might not wear a cape or shoot laser beams from its eyes, but it does bring some unique qualities to the table. Let's dive into how this superhero mingles with other philosophical and spiritual heavyweights, finding common ground and grappling with differences.

Secular Buddhism is a no-nonsense, pragmatic approach to life, focusing on understanding reality, the human mind, and suffering through critical inquiry and empirical evidence. Unlike traditional religious doctrines, secular Buddhism prefers a hands-on, evidence-based approach. It's like the Sherlock Holmes of spirituality, investigating life's mysteries with a magnifying glass and a penchant for critical thinking.

On the flip side, many spiritual and philosophical traditions come with a side of supernatural or religious dressing. They might believe in higher powers, souls, or spirits, but their goal is often similar: helping people make sense of life and find meaning in the chaos.

Now, you might think secular Buddhism and these other philosophies would be like oil and water, never mixing. But surprise, surprise! They can actually complement each other in some fascinating ways. Many people find practices like meditation, mindfulness, and contemplation appealing, no matter their spiritual background. It's like a philosophical potluck, where everyone brings their favorite dish to share.

Moreover, secular Buddhism's practical, evidence-based approach can add some much-needed grounding to other spiritual traditions. It's like a bridge between science and spirituality, enabling people to explore their inner workings and the nature of existence with both feet firmly planted on the ground.

However, the journey isn't all sunshine and rainbows. Secular Buddhism and other philosophies can diverge in some pretty significant ways. For example, some traditional religions believe that humans are fundamentally flawed and need salvation from a higher power. Secular Buddhism, on the other hand, believes that we can train our minds to overcome suffering and cultivate compassion and wisdom, all on our own. It's like a spiritual DIY project, with no divine intervention required.

To sum it up, secular Buddhism is like a philosophical superhero, making friends and facing off with other spiritual and philosophical traditions. With its unique blend of practicality, critical inquiry, and evidence-based thinking, secular Buddhism can both complement and challenge other perspectives. Together, they form a diverse tapestry of ideas, helping us all grapple with life's big questions and find meaning in the chaos.

Secular Buddhism: A Hilarious Guide to the Perks and Pitfalls of a No-Nonsense Spiritual Path

Embracing a secular Buddhist perspective is like signing up for a spiritual gym membership, complete with sweaty workouts and potential muscle gains (minus the protein shakes). This no-nonsense approach to Buddhism is winning hearts, but it's not all zen and unicorns. Let's take a look at the perks and pitfalls of jumping on the secular Buddhism bandwagon.

First up, the perks! By adopting a secular Buddhist perspective, you'll be training in the art of mindfulness and compassion. Think of it as emotional bodybuilding, where you flex your empathy muscles and bulk up on self-awareness. The result? Reduced stress and improved relationships – all without a single trip to the gym.

Another perk is the freedom to be a spiritual rebel. Secular Buddhism encourages questioning everything, including the Buddha himself. It's like being a punk rocker of the philosophical world – you can toss out dogma and embrace intellectual freedom, leading to greater personal growth.

But wait, there's a flip side to this spiritual coin. One potential pitfall of secular Buddhism is that it might lead to sidelining traditional aspects of Buddhism, like religious rituals and texts. By focusing only on the practical, you might miss out on some spiritual gems hidden in the more mystical corners of Buddhism.

And here's the kicker: adopting a secular Buddhist perspective comes with the need for ongoing self-reflection and commitment to personal growth. You can't just sit back and bask in your newfound mindfulness. No, siree! You've got to face your flaws, question your beliefs, and constantly strive for self-improvement. It's like signing up for a never-ending spiritual marathon, but the finish line is personal growth.

In a nutshell, embracing secular Buddhism has its perks and pitfalls. You get to flex your mindfulness muscles, cultivate compassion, and be a spiritual rebel, but it comes with the cost of ongoing self-reflection and commitment to personal growth. So, before you dive into the secular Buddhist pool, make sure you're ready to face the challenges (and maybe pack some floaties, just in case).

Stories and reflections that inspire others to forge their own paths.

For many years, I felt lost and unfulfilled, searching for some sense of purpose and meaning in life. It wasn't until I discovered secular Buddhism that I was able to make sense of it all.

At first, I was skeptical. I had always thought of Buddhism as a religion with a set of strict rules and rituals to follow. But as I began to learn more about secular Buddhism, I realized that it was an entirely different approach to life.

Rather than focusing on religious beliefs, secular Buddhism emphasizes the practical application of Buddhist principles to our everyday lives.

Through my practice of secular Buddhism, I have learned to cultivate mindfulness, compassion, and wisdom. I have learned to embrace impermanence and accept the uncertain nature of life. I have found peace and contentment in the present moment, rather than constantly striving for more.

The most profound lesson I have learned is that happiness comes from within. It's something we can cultivate through our own efforts, rather than something we have to seek from external sources. By letting go of attachment and embracing the present moment, we can find true fulfillment and meaning.

Another individual I know, who found solace in secular Buddhism, had been grappling with anxiety and a lingering sense of dissatisfaction. Despite a successful career and a loving family, they felt something was missing. That's when they stumbled upon secular Buddhism, and it felt like they had finally found the missing piece of the puzzle.

Initially, they had reservations about the spiritual aspect of Buddhism, but secular Buddhism's emphasis on practicality and evidence-based thinking resonated with them. They started practicing mindfulness meditation and noticed a significant reduction in their anxiety levels. They also began to appreciate the small moments of joy in their daily lives, something they had previously overlooked.

One of the key takeaways from their journey was the understanding that happiness is not a destination, but rather a skill that can be cultivated through practice. By embracing secular Buddhist principles, they learned to navigate life's challenges with grace and resilience. They also discovered the power of compassionate action and its impact on their own well-being.

The support and camaraderie found in the secular Buddhist community were instrumental in their personal growth. They witnessed firsthand the power of connection and shared experiences in overcoming obstacles and fostering a deeper understanding of life's complexities.

For those seeking their own paths, the personal stories and reflections of individuals who have found meaning and fulfillment through secular Buddhism can serve as sources of inspiration and encouragement. By exploring secular Buddhist principles and practices, you may find the tools and insights needed to transform your life, foster inner peace, and experience lasting happiness.

CHAPTER 10

Basking in the Warmth of Gratitude and Contentment

Gratitude: A Secret Ingredient for a Supercharged Life

Have you ever stopped to think about what would happen if you injected a dose of gratitude into your daily routine? Well, buckle up, my secular Buddhist friend, because we're about to embark on a wild ride through the land of appreciation and its mind-boggling impact on our well-being.

Gratitude, the art of high-fiving life for all the awesome stuff it throws our way, is the ultimate mood booster. Think of it as your brain's personal DJ, spinning happy tunes and cranking up those dopamine and serotonin levels for a non-stop feel-good party.

But wait, there's more! Gratitude is like a pair of rose-tinted glasses, helping us see the world in a whole new light. Suddenly, those mundane moments become epic adventures, and life's little hiccups transform into opportunities for growth. Talk about a 180-degree turn in perspective!

And what's a good party without some social mingling? Gratitude's got you covered there, too. By showing appreciation for the people in our lives, we're not only scoring brownie points but also building solid connections. We become expert forgivers and unleash our inner social butterflies, making our relationships flourish like never before.

So, what's the secret to unlocking this gratitude-powered life upgrade? It's simple: whether it's journaling, meditation, or daily shoutouts to the universe, find your own gratitude groove and watch the magic unfold. In a world where negativity often takes center stage, embracing gratitude can be a game-changer, helping you live a life that's happier, healthier, and more fulfilling. So go ahead, give gratitude a go, and witness your secular Buddhist journey become a whole lot more enjoyable!

How to Grow a Gratitude Garden: Planting Seeds of Appreciation in Everyday Life

Feeling ready to add some gratitude into your life? Great! Let's dive into some tried-and-true strategies that'll have you saying "Thank you, universe!" in no time.

1. The Gratitude Diaries: Jot down your daily wins in a gratitude journal, from that scrumptious breakfast to your comfy bed. The more you write, the more you'll realize how much there is to be grateful for. It's like a happiness scavenger hunt!

2. Celebrate the Little Things: Keep an eye out for tiny treasures sprinkled throughout your day. Did you get the last parking spot? Score! Did someone hold the elevator for you? Hooray! Life's full of little victories just waiting to be appreciated.

3. Mindfulness: Unleash Your Inner Zen Master: Carve out a few moments each day to practice mindfulness meditation. By tuning into the here and now, you'll uncover hidden gems of gratitude lurking in plain sight.

4. Karma in Action: Roll up your sleeves and give back to your community. Volunteering not only helps others but also helps you appreciate the good stuff in your life. Plus, it's a great way to meet other gratitude enthusiasts!

5. Say "Thanks" Like You Mean It: Whether it's a hug, a thank-you note, or a heartfelt high-five, make sure you let the people in your life know how much you appreciate them. They'll feel great, and so will you!

By nurturing these gratitude seeds in your daily life, you'll soon have a thriving garden of appreciation that'll make your secular Buddhist journey an absolute delight. Happy gratitude growing!

Gratitude and Contentment: The Dynamic Duo of Happiness

Picture this: gratitude and contentment, two superheroes of the emotional world, teaming up to supercharge your happiness. How, you ask? Well, let's take a closer look at this dynamic duo and the power they wield when they join forces.

Gratitude, the act of counting our blessings, can be the ultimate sidekick to contentment, our trusty companion in feeling satisfied with life. When we're grateful, we're more likely to kick discontent to the curb and appreciate what we have. It's like gratitude puts on its rose-colored glasses and whispers, "Hey, things are pretty great, aren't they?"

Now, let's flip the script. Contentment, the zen master of satisfaction, can give gratitude a boost by keeping us grounded in the present moment. When we're content, we become mindful superheroes, noticing all the good stuff we might've overlooked before. Suddenly, we're dishing out thank-yous left and right!

It's a beautiful cycle, really: gratitude begets contentment, which in turn fuels more gratitude. Together, they create a powerhouse of positivity that can make our lives more joyful and fulfilling.

So, why not invite this dynamic duo into your life? Practice gratitude, embrace contentment, and watch as they reinforce each other to transform your secular Buddhist journey into a whirlwind of happiness. Trust me; it's a partnership you won't want to miss out on!

Gratitude Roadblocks: Dodging the Hurdles on Your Path to Happiness

Let's face it: practicing gratitude can be like running an obstacle course. But fear not, my secular Buddhist friends! I'm here to help you navigate those pesky hurdles so you can bask in the glow of gratitude.

1. The Negativity Monster: Tired of dwelling in the shadow of negative thoughts? Time to show them who's boss! Whenever you catch yourself getting dragged down, flip the script and focus on something positive. Bonus points for jotting them down in your shiny new gratitude journal!

2. The Comparison Trap: Feeling like everyone else is living their best life while you're stuck in the slow lane? Put the brakes on those comparisons! Celebrate your own victories (no matter how small) and cheer on your personal growth.

3. The Busy Bee Dilemma: Always buzzing around, never stopping to smell the roses? Schedule a gratitude pit stop in your daily routine. Whether it's five minutes of reflection before bed or a quick lunchtime gratitude blitz, make time for a little thankfulness.

4. The Vulnerability Vortex: Afraid that embracing gratitude means letting down your guard? Ease into it with baby steps. Thank a colleague for their help, or take a moment to admire a beautiful sunset. Before you know it, you'll be a gratitude pro!

5. The Obliviousness Obstacle: Can't see the forest for the trees when it comes to gratitude? Time to sharpen your awareness skills! Practice mindfulness to help you spot those hidden gems of gratitude lurking all around you.

In a world riddled with gratitude roadblocks, it's crucial to stay on track and keep your eyes on the prize. Remember, you've got the power to conquer these obstacles and make gratitude a staple of your daily life. Happy hurdling!

The Perks of Contentment: How to Live Your Best Life by Embracing Satisfaction

Picture this: you're living your best life, stress-free, and filled with happiness, all thanks to contentment. Sounds like a dream, right? Well, it's not just a fantasy! Practicing contentment comes with some serious perks, including increased satisfaction with life and reduced stress. So, buckle up, and let's dive into the wonderful world of contentment.

Life Satisfaction Level-Up

Embracing contentment can be like finding the secret cheat code to life satisfaction. Focusing on the treasures you already possess, rather than the ones that elude you, can boost your gratitude and joy levels. With this power-up, you'll be well on your way to conquering the game of life.

Stress-Busting Superpowers

Sick of stress holding you hostage? Contentment to the rescue! By hitting the pause button on your never-ending quest for more, you can bid farewell to anxiety and stress. Say hello to a life filled with inner peace and sweet, sweet serenity.

Relationship Boosters

Contentment isn't just a solo mission – it can enhance your relationships too! When you're at peace with yourself, jealousy and envy won't stand a chance. Instead, you'll be cheering on your loved ones and basking in their successes. High fives all around!

Financial Ninja Skills

Get ready to unlock your inner financial ninja with contentment as your sensei. By being satisfied with your current loot, you'll dodge the pitfalls of overspending on frivolous items. Master the art of saving and investing in experiences that truly matter.

In a nutshell, contentment offers a treasure trove of benefits that can elevate your life to new heights. So, embrace satisfaction, and watch as your life transforms into a happier, more peaceful, and fulfilled adventure. Contentment, assemble!

Unleashing Contentment: A User's Guide to Living in the Now and Loving It

Ah, contentment – that elusive state of mind where we're perfectly happy with the here and now. Sounds like a dream, doesn't it? Well, fear not, dear reader! With these techniques, you can become a contentment connoisseur and enjoy the sweet taste of satisfaction.

1. Master the art of "Now": Want to know the secret ingredient for contentment? It's savoring the present moment. Don't let your past regrets or future worries spoil the dish. Instead, indulge in the flavors of the present moment and focus on the experiences that surround you.

2. Mindfulness: Your Contentment Superpower: Channel your inner mindfulness superhero to help cultivate contentment. Keep an eye on your thoughts and emotions, but don't get too attached – you're just a friendly observer. With this newfound power, you'll develop a serene and peaceful mind.

3. A Daily Dose of Gratitude: Gratitude is like adding a dash of extra spice to your contentment recipe. Spend a few minutes each day jotting down what you're thankful for. Focusing on life's positives will help you whip up an attitude of appreciation.

4. Tame the Expectation Beast: Expectations can be sneaky creatures, leading to disappointment and frustration. Learn to let go of expectations and embrace the art of acceptance. Stay goal-oriented, but be flexible and adaptable in your journey.

5. Delight in Life's Simple Pleasures: Believe it or not, contentment can be found in the tiniest of moments. Learn to relish life's simple pleasures, like cuddling with a loved one or marveling at a stunning sunset.

In a nutshell, cultivating contentment is an adventure that requires time, patience, and a hearty appetite for happiness. By practicing these techniques, you can savor the flavors of contentment and experience a life filled with joy, peace, and fulfillment. Bon appétit!

The Dynamic Duo of Mental Health: Gratitude and Contentment

In the grand adventure of life, two superheroes come to the rescue of your mental well-being: Gratitude and Contentment! These formidable allies are essential for maintaining long-term happiness and keeping those dastardly villains, like stress and anxiety, at bay.

Gratitude, the mighty appreciator, has the power to make you feel thankful for life's good things, no matter how tiny they might be. Contentment, the zen master, helps you find satisfaction and acceptance in your current life without the constant yearning for more. Together, they form a dynamic duo that fosters positivity, resilience, and happiness.

By practicing gratitude and contentment, you can train your mind to focus on the bright side, even when dark clouds roll in. These superpowers can improve your relationships, boost life satisfaction, and enhance your connection to the world.

But wait, there's more! Gratitude and contentment's effects go beyond fleeting happiness. Research shows that those who regularly tap into these powers experience lower stress and depression levels, better sleep quality, and stronger immune systems. They also enjoy a greater sense of social connectedness, a vital ingredient for mental well-being.

In summary, gratitude and contentment are the dynamic duo you need to maintain mental well-being and long-term happiness. Make them a regular part of your daily life to cultivate a positive attitude, strengthen your resilience, and vanquish those mental health villains. With Gratitude and Contentment by your side, you're well on your way to living your happiest, healthiest life!

CHAPTER 11

Breaking Up is Hard to Do: Building Healthy Relationships through Secular Buddhism

Unearthing the laughably simple secrets of Secular Buddhism for flourishing relationships: mindfulness, compassion, and non-attachment, oh my!

Have you ever wondered how Secular Buddhism, the spiritual philosophy that's like the laid-back cousin of traditional Buddhism, can help you transform your relationships into love fests? The answer lies in three hilarious yet effective principles: mindfulness, compassion, and non-attachment.

Mindfulness is like the quirky best friend who reminds you to pay attention to the present moment, without judgment. It's a practice that helps you tune into your own thoughts and feelings, as well as the emotions of those around you. And guess what? It turns out that being more mindful can make you a communication wizard, with the power to forge stronger bonds with your fellow humans.

Next up is compassion, the superhero of empathy. Compassion swoops in to recognize and understand the suffering of others, giving them a soft landing when they need it most. It's about being kind to others, even if they've stepped on your toes (literally or metaphorically) or have a different outlook on life. Developing compassion is like spinning a web of meaningful connections that creates a warm and fuzzy sense of community.

Finally, we have non-attachment – the art of not clinging to stuff, status, or expectations like a desperate limpet. Non-attachment teaches us that everything has an expiration date, and it's best not to get too hung up on the future or the past. By embracing non-attachment, your relationships will be built on a solid foundation of mutual respect, rather than shallow values or expectations.

In a nutshell, Secular Buddhism's principles are like a magical recipe for healthier, happier relationships. By sprinkling mindfulness, compassion, and non-attachment into your daily life, you'll be on the fast track to creating deeper connections with both yourself and others. So, buckle up and enjoy the ride to a more fulfilling life with your newfound Secular Buddhist wisdom!

Say "Hello" to mindfulness – your new relationship BFF that helps you become a communication and conflict resolution ninja!

Picture this: you're in the middle of a disagreement with your significant other or friend, and things are getting heated. Suddenly, mindfulness enters the scene, ready to save the day with its trusty sidekicks, active listening and empathetic understanding.

Let's start with active listening, the superhero of communication skills. Instead of interrupting or zoning out when someone else is talking, active listening is all about giving them the stage and the spotlight. By putting our thoughts and feelings on hold, we're able to genuinely understand what's going on in the other person's head. It's like being a mind reader, without the need for a crystal ball or a psychic hotline!

Now, let's introduce empathetic understanding, the conflict resolution guru. This skill is all about slipping into the other person's shoes and seeing the world from their point of view (even if it's a little uncomfortable or tight). By doing so, we're able to empathize with their situation, preventing petty arguments from morphing into Godzilla-sized conflicts.

Becoming a mindfulness master won't happen faster than you can say "om," but with practice, patience, and a dash of vulnerability, you'll be well on your way to transforming your relationships. So, get ready to unlock the power of mindfulness and make your communication and conflict resolution skills the envy of everyone you know!

Say goodbye to your ego: embracing the hilarious wisdom of Buddhism's "non-self" to supercharge your connection with others!

Picture your ego as a stubborn mule that always wants to be the center of attention. Now, imagine the enlightening concept of "non-self" in Buddhism coming to the rescue, helping you send that attention-seeking mule packing!

Buddhism's non-self concept suggests that we're not a permanent, unchanging self or soul. Instead, we're a beautiful collage of ever-changing, interdependent elements that include our bodies, thoughts, and emotions. This idea might seem as puzzling as a Rubik's Cube, but once you crack the code, you'll see a world of interdependence and interconnectedness.

By embracing non-self, we can finally deflate our ego and stop wrestling for the spotlight. We'll start to see that our happiness is hilariously intertwined with the well-being of others. This realization leads to a compassion explosion, as we become more empathetic and understanding.

Kicking ego-driven behaviors to the curb takes time, patience, and practice. But by questioning our beliefs about selfhood and identity, we can open our minds to new ways of thinking and connecting. So, buckle up and embark on a journey toward a more fulfilling life with the wisdom of non-self guiding you all the way!

Laugh your way to a love fest with compassion: the secret sauce for healthy relationships with yourself and others!

Compassion is the heartwarming ingredient that makes relationships flourish like a blooming flower. It's all about empathizing with others' challenges and showing them we care. And, just like the perfect dance routine, compassion involves a two-step process: being kind to yourself and extending that kindness to others.

First, let's talk about self-compassion – giving yourself a bear hug when life throws you curveballs. It's all about acknowledging your feelings, wrapping yourself in a cozy blanket of understanding, and being your own best friend. Mastering the art of self-compassion means you'll not only treat yourself better, but you'll also create a foundation for better relationships with others. Because let's face it, if you can't be kind to yourself, how can you be kind to others?

Next up is extending compassion to others, the relationship equivalent of a warm cup of cocoa on a chilly day. It means stepping into another person's shoes (without tripping), understanding their point of view, and offering support. This magical elixir of empathy deepens connections, encourages open communication, and creates an atmosphere of trust and respect.

But wait, there's more! Compassion doesn't just help your relationships – it's also a wellness booster. Studies show that compassionate folks enjoy lower stress levels, better emotional balance, and improved overall health. It's like a triple-whammy of awesomeness!

So, let's raise a toast to compassion – the secret sauce that makes our relationships healthier, happier, and more harmonious. By cultivating self-compassion and extending it to others, you'll be on your way to creating the loving connections you've always dreamed of. Cheers to that!

Rolling with the punches: using non-attachment and acceptance to surf the waves of relationship challenges and change like a boss!

Picture non-attachment and acceptance as your personal relationship superheroes, swooping in to help you navigate the twists and turns of your love life. Non-attachment is the art of letting go of expectations, while acceptance is the practice of embracing reality with open arms. Together, they're a dynamic duo that can help you stay on your feet when life throws relationship curveballs.

Relationship challenges are like roller coaster rides – thrilling, scary, and full of ups and downs. Whether it's heated arguments, heart-wrenching breakups, or other bumpy patches, these challenges can stir up a whirlwind of emotions. Non-attachment helps you step back from the emotional storm, clearing your mind and allowing you to tackle the situation with grace and humor.

Acceptance plays a starring role in overcoming relationship challenges too. It's all about facing the reality of a situation, even when it's as tough as an overcooked steak. By embracing what's happening, you can find peace of mind and make more informed decisions. Plus, accepting the ever-changing nature of relationships helps you remain open to new experiences and opportunities for growth.

But that's not all! Non-attachment and acceptance are also your go-to sidekicks when dealing with change. Change can be as tricky as a greased pig, but these principles help you work through the emotional hurdles that often tag along. Instead of clinging to the past like a toddler to a favorite toy, you can move forward with a spirit of curiosity and adaptability.

In a nutshell, non-attachment and acceptance are your secret weapons for navigating relationship challenges and changes with ease. By adopting these principles, you can lead a more resilient, fulfilling life – and tackle whatever curveballs come your way with a smile and a wink!

Embracing the mantra of owning our actions and emotions in relationships: ditching the blame game and steering clear of manipulation!

In the world of relationships, taking responsibility for our own actions and emotions is like putting on a cape and transforming into a superhero. It's the key to creating healthy, loving partnerships that thrive. After all, who wants to be stuck in a blame game or a tangled web of manipulation?

When we point fingers and blame our partners, we're doing more harm than good. Nobody likes to be on the receiving end of a constant barrage of accusations or feel like they're always walking on eggshells. So, let's put the blame game in the trash bin and take responsibility for our actions – because that's where true relationship magic happens!

Owning our emotions is just as important as taking responsibility for our actions. It's like opening the door to a world of trust and clear communication. When we're honest about our feelings, we create a cozy, safe space where both partners can speak their minds and work through issues together.

To sum it up, taking responsibility for our actions and emotions in a relationship is like hitting the jackpot. It paves the way for healthy communication, trust, and mutual respect. Blaming or manipulating our partner is a one-way ticket to Relationship Doomsville, so let's embrace accountability and build partnerships based on love, honesty, and understanding. Now, that's a recipe for relationship success!

Sprinkling humor and secular Buddhist principles into relationship-strengthening exercises and meditations – because who doesn't want a relationship that's a real barrel of laughs?

Relationships are like plants; they need care and attention to grow and flourish. And what better way to keep them healthy than by adding a pinch of secular Buddhist principles and a dash of laughter? Here are some practical exercises and meditations to bring your relationships to the next level – and keep them there!

The art of hilarious listening: Communication is the lifeblood of any relationship. To spice things up, try practicing mindful listening with a twist – share funny stories, jokes, or even impersonate your favorite cartoon characters. The key is to pay attention to what your partner is saying and have fun while doing it!

The "laughing-kindness" meditation: Swap out the traditional loving-kindness meditation for a "laughing-kindness" version. Sit comfortably and close your eyes. As you breathe in and out, imagine sending out waves of laughter and joy to yourself, your partner, and the world. It's a recipe for instant happiness!

The self-reflection chuckle: Get to know yourself and your needs with a side of humor. Reflect on your quirks, funny habits, and even your most amusing relationship blunders. Embracing self-awareness with a smile can make you a better and more understanding partner.

Gratitude with giggles: Jot down a list of things you appreciate about your partner – including their ability to make you laugh. Share your list and enjoy the warm fuzzies (and chuckles) that follow.

Mindful chit-chat: Remember, mindful communication is the secret sauce in any relationship. So why not sprinkle in some laughter? While staying present and compassionate, weave humor into your conversations. Laughter can defuse tension and help you both feel more connected.

By blending secular Buddhist principles, meditation, and a healthy dose of humor, you'll be well on your way to building and maintaining relationships that are both meaningful and hilariously fun. So go ahead, laugh, love, and live mindfully – together!

CHAPTER 12

Juggling the Inner and Outer Worlds: Balancing Inner Peace and Outer Responsibilities

The Great Juggling Act: Balancing Your Inner and Outer Worlds for Personal Growth and a Barrel of Laughs

Imagine your life as a circus act where you're the world's most amazing juggler, keeping your inner and outer worlds up in the air in a graceful dance. Your inner world is the elephant on the unicycle, representing your emotions, thoughts, and beliefs, while your outer world is the mischievous monkey on the trapeze—your physical surroundings and social interactions.

Too often, we focus on the elephant, letting the monkey swing out of control or vice versa, which leads to a topsy-turvy circus where nobody's laughing, and we end up feeling as disconnected as a clown without a red nose. Not the best show on Earth, eh?

The key to personal growth and development is turning our circus into a hilarious, well-coordinated performance by finding the sweet spot between our unicycle-riding elephant and high-flying monkey. When we give each the attention they deserve, we create a harmonious environment where we can find joy and fulfillment.

Focusing on our inner elephant helps us master our emotions and thoughts, leading to healthier relationships with ourselves and others. But if we let our monkey run amok, we risk losing sight of our values and purpose, getting lost in a jungle of distractions.

So, step right up and prepare for the great balancing act of your life! It might take time and practice, but once you achieve this equilibrium, you'll be the ringmaster of your own happiness and have a truly spectacular show that even the toughest critics will applaud.

The Inner World Adventure: Delving into the Wild and Wacky World of Thoughts, Feelings, Beliefs, and Values

Picture your inner world as an undiscovered land filled with peculiar creatures: thoughts, feelings, beliefs, and values, all roaming around, shaping your perception of the outer world like a kaleidoscope of adventure. Understanding this colorful realm is like finding the treasure map to a meaningful and fulfilling life—X marks the spot!

First, let's meet the thoughts—those curious critters that can either lift our spirits or lead us down a rabbit hole of doom and gloom. They're the backbone of our emotions and behaviors, and they love to play dress-up, taking on positive or negative disguises. A positive thought can be a ray of sunshine, while a negative one might resemble a grumpy raincloud.

Next, we encounter the wise old owls—our beliefs and values. Perched high in the trees, they shape our attitudes, opinions, and how we navigate life's twists and turns. For example, an owl that values honesty will hoot disapprovingly at any sign of corruption.

Now, let's not forget how our inner world responds to external stimuli. When the creatures of our inner world encounter events from the outer world, they form a unique response team. Understanding these quirky patterns of behavior and identifying triggers helps us develop strategies to manage stress and conflicts like a cool, cucumber-wielding cowboy.

Embarking on the quest to understand our inner world is a wild and wacky ride, but it's key to personal growth and self-improvement. As we become more aware of our own mental menagerie, we can align our behavior with our true selves, fostering positive change in our lives and the world beyond. So, grab your safari hat and start exploring!

The Outer World Extravaganza: Embracing the Surroundings, Relationships, and Experiences of Our Wild and Wonderful World

Picture your outer world as a vibrant carnival, complete with whirling rides, fascinating characters, and thrilling experiences. Understanding this wacky wonderland is essential because it influences our inner world and shapes our daily lives in countless ways.

First, let's talk about the set design—the physical environment that surrounds us. Our surroundings can be like a roller coaster, lifting our spirits or sending them plummeting. A cluttered workspace can make us feel like we're stuck in a hall of mirrors, disoriented and unproductive. But spending time in nature can refresh us like a leisurely ride on the Ferris wheel, boosting focus and melting away negativity. By grasping the impact of our surroundings, we can choose environments that set the stage for a show-stopping performance.

Next, we have the diverse cast of characters—our relationships with others. These interactions can either feel like a heartwarming hug from a favorite mascot or the dreaded spinning teacups ride that leaves us queasy. Nurturing positive relationships can turn life into a delightful parade, while negative connections can leave us feeling stuck on a never-ending loop of the Gravitron. By recognizing how relationships affect our well-being, we can invest in the ones that bring sunshine to our carnival.

Finally, we can't forget about the wild experiences that make up the outer world's roller coaster of life. Challenges, accomplishments, and setbacks are the twists and turns that shape our inner world, inspiring growth or reinforcing limiting beliefs. By understanding these experiences, we can learn from them and develop new perspectives to conquer future rides with flair.

In the end, embracing the outer world's extravagant carnival helps us shape our inner world. Our environment, relationships, and experiences have a tremendous impact on our behavior and emotional state. By reflecting on these aspects, we can make informed decisions about how to live our lives, turning our personal carnival into a place of wonder, joy, and well-being.

The Art of Balancing: Fun and Quirky Tips for Harmonizing Your Inner and Outer Worlds

Finding balance between your inner and outer worlds can feel like trying to walk a tightrope while juggling flaming torches. Fear not! Here are some entertaining yet practical tips and exercises to help you master this daring act:

Embrace Mindfulness: Mindfulness is like a backstage pass to the present moment, keeping you fully engaged and in tune with your thoughts, feelings, and sensations. Try practices like mindful breathing, body scans, or mindful moonwalking (or regular walking, if you're not feeling as groovy). Set aside a few minutes each day to be fully present.

Meditate Like a Zen Master: Meditation is like a magical potion that calms your mind, melts away stress, and makes you feel like you're floating on a cloud of well-being. Find a quiet spot, get comfy, and focus on your breath. Or, try guided meditations from apps or online resources—think of them as your personal meditation DJs.

Write It Out: Journaling is like having a heart-to-heart with your inner self. Penning your thoughts, emotions, and experiences can help you uncover insights and solve the mysteries of your own personal universe. Set aside time each day to spill your innermost secrets onto paper.

Draw Boundaries Like a Pro: Think of setting boundaries as designing your personal blueprint for a balanced life. Lay down the groundwork by saying no when necessary, establishing realistic expectations, and communicating your needs like a skilled architect.

Treat Yo' Self: Self-care is the secret sauce for finding balance between your inner and outer worlds. Whip up a batch by mixing in exercise, healthy eating, nature walks, hobbies, and quality time with loved ones.

Remember, achieving balance is an ongoing process, like learning to ride a unicycle. By practicing mindfulness, meditating, journaling, setting boundaries, and indulging in self-care, you'll soon become the ringmaster of your own harmonious circus.

Juggling Life's Curveballs: Tackling Obstacles to Inner and Outer World Harmony with Humor and Grace

Life can feel like a comedy of errors, with obstacles like negative self-talk, societal expectations, and external pressures trying to steal the show. Fear not! With a dash of humor and grace, you can overcome these pesky hurdles and harmonize your inner and outer worlds. Let's take a closer look at these stage-crashing culprits and how to handle them like a pro.

Negative Self-Talk: The Inner Heckler

Negative self-talk is like that annoying heckler at a comedy show, constantly criticizing and undermining you. It's time to silence this inner critic and turn the spotlight on your strengths.

To outwit your inner heckler, become aware of these self-critical thoughts and challenge them with a witty comeback. Swap out negative self-talk for applause-worthy affirmations, like "I'm more than enough" or "I've got talent to spare!"

Societal Expectations: The Unrealistic Script

Society hands us a script filled with unrealistic expectations about looks, success, and behavior. It's time to toss that old script and write a new one that stars the real you.

To rewrite your life's script, recognize those expectations and challenge them with your own unique qualities and strengths. Remember, your worth isn't determined by box office numbers or the size of your dressing room—it's defined by the authentic you.

External Pressures: The Demanding Director

External pressures, like work, finances, or family obligations, can feel like a demanding director shouting, "Do more! Be more!" It's time to turn down the volume on these pressures and take a well-deserved intermission.

To ease the stress of external pressures, make self-care your encore. Prioritize activities that bring laughter and relaxation, set boundaries, and learn to say no without guilt. Remember, you're the star of your show, and you deserve a standing ovation for taking care of yourself.

In conclusion, harmonizing your inner and outer worlds might feel like a high-wire act, but with self-awareness, humor, and grace, you'll be the ringmaster of your own balanced life. Tackle those obstacles with a smile, and soon you'll be taking your final bow to thunderous applause.

Self-Care: The Secret Sauce to Inner and Outer World Harmony

Self-care is like a secret sauce that adds zest to our lives and helps us maintain a scrumptious balance between our inner and outer worlds. It's all about indulging in activities that nourish our physical, mental, and emotional health.

In the hustle and bustle of life, we sometimes forget to treat ourselves to a self-care appetizer. But fear not, we've cooked up a delightful menu of self-care activities that'll keep you satisfied and balanced.

Exercise: The Energizing Entrée

Exercise is like an invigorating entrée that boosts your physical health while spicing up your mood. Whether you're stretching your limbs with yoga, taking a leisurely walk, or dancing your heart out, exercise is the perfect recipe for reducing stress and anxiety.

Healthy Eating: The Nutritious Nourishment

Whipping up a healthy meal is like mixing the perfect ingredients for a balanced life. A nutritious diet, filled with whole grains, fruits, veggies, lean protein, and healthy fats, is essential for keeping your energy levels high and your body in tip-top shape.

Hobbies: The Flavorful Fun

Every good meal needs a side of fun, and that's where hobbies come in. Hobbies add flavor to life, reduce stress, and tickle our creativity taste buds. Whether you're painting a masterpiece or penning a novel, hobbies are a delectable way to improve your mental and emotional health.

Relaxation Techniques: The Soothing Sweets

And finally, the pièce de résistance—relaxation techniques. These are the sweet treats that melt stress away and help us savor the moment. Deep breathing, meditation, or a simple pause in your day can help calm your mind and sprinkle your life with tranquility.

So self-care is the mouthwatering secret sauce that helps us maintain a healthy balance between our inner and outer worlds. By savoring activities like exercise, healthy eating, hobbies, and relaxation techniques, we can cook up a life that's both nutritious and delicious. So, bon appétit to a balanced and fulfilling life!

Exploring and Growing Your Personal Development Journey

In conclusion, balancing our inner and outer worlds is essential to leading a healthy, fulfilled, and well-rounded life. Some key points discussed in this chapter include understanding the importance of our inner world, which is made up of our thoughts, feelings, beliefs, and values, as well as the outer world, which encompasses our surroundings, relationships, and experiences. We have also touched upon the need to find balance through mindfulness practices, setting boundaries, and overcoming obstacles like negative self-talk, societal expectations, and external pressures.

Moreover, we have emphasized the importance of self-care in maintaining a healthy balance between our inner and outer worlds, with examples like exercise, healthy eating, and hobbies. By taking these points into consideration and putting them into practice, we can work towards achieving a harmonious balance in our lives.

We encourage you, as readers, to take steps towards balancing your inner and outer worlds by incorporating the tips and exercises discussed in this chapter. Continue exploring and growing in your personal development journey, remaining open to new experiences and constantly learning about yourself. By doing so, you will create a life filled with purpose, meaning, and true happiness.

CHAPTER 13

Diving Deep into Your Spirituality: Deepening Your Spiritual Practice

The Art of Spiritual Stick-to-itiveness.

Consistency, the secret sauce of spiritual growth, is the backbone of a flourishing Secular Buddhist practice. It's the trusty sidekick that keeps you on track, nudging you to meditate even when you'd rather binge-watch your favorite TV series.

Picture this: you're all fired up to start your spiritual journey. You're meditating like a champ, chanting your heart out, and feeling all Zen. But then, life happens—work piles up, your cat develops an odd fascination with your meditation cushion, and your enthusiasm wanes. Sounds familiar?

Well, fret not, fellow spiritual explorers! Consistency is here to save the day. It's like a gym buddy, but for your soul. Consistency keeps you disciplined and builds habits that stick, turning your spiritual practice into a piece of cake (or tofu, if that's more your style).

But wait, there's more! Consistency lays the groundwork for your spiritual superhighway. With regular practice, you'll forge an unshakable connection to the divine, honing your intuition and discovering the spiritual equivalent of buried treasure—insights, experiences, and inner peace galore.

And let's not forget the cherry on top: commitment. Sticking to your practice, even when you'd rather sleep in or go out for happy hour, sends a powerful message to yourself and the universe. It's like shouting, "Hey, I'm serious about this spiritual gig!" Your unwavering dedication helps you inch closer to a life filled with joy, purpose, and the warm fuzzies that come from living true to your values.

In a nutshell, consistency is the MVP of spiritual growth. It's the key to discipline, habit formation, and a rock-solid spiritual foundation. So, grab your spiritual sneakers and let's make consistency our BFF on this journey towards a more fulfilling, Secular Buddhist life!

The Spiritual Buffet

Like a smorgasbord of delicious practices, spirituality offers a veritable feast of ways to connect with your inner Zen master. Meditation, prayer, yoga, and mindfulness are just a few of the tantalizing options up for grabs.

Spirituality is like a choose-your-own-adventure novel, with each person taking a unique path toward meaning and purpose. Forget the one-size-fits-all approach of organized religion—why not try on a variety of spiritual hats and see which one fits like a glove?

Meditation, the spiritual world's version of a power nap, is a great place to start. Just plop down, focus on your breath, and let your inner peace-o-meter skyrocket. You'll be cruising through stress-free lanes, waving goodbye to anxiety and mental fog in no time.

Not feeling the quiet vibes? Give prayer a whirl! Chat with the universe (or any higher power of your choice) and watch as your gratitude meter and connection to the world around you soar. It's like having a direct line to celestial customer service, available 24/7.

If stretching is more your style, then roll out a yoga mat and let the spiritual pretzel-making commence! With its combo of physical postures, breathing exercises, and meditation, yoga is like the Swiss Army knife of spiritual practices. Prepare to feel grounded, centered, and best buds with your body.

Last but not least, mindfulness is the hot new kid on the spiritual block. It's all about living in the now, soaking up the present moment like a sponge, and bidding adieu to judgment and distraction. Hello, calmness, and connection!

The bottom line? Spirituality is a journey of self-discovery, and there's no right or wrong way to explore the menu. So, dive into the spiritual buffet, sampling the delightful array of practices until you find the perfect combo that tantalizes your soul. Mix and match, experiment, and remember that this journey is all about finding what resonates with you. After all, the beauty of spirituality lies in its diversity, like a patchwork quilt of meaningful experiences tailored just for you. So, grab a fork, and let the spiritual feast begin!

Join the Spiritual Squad

Picture this—you're on an epic spiritual journey, but at times, it feels like you're trekking solo through the wilderness. The solution? Finding your tribe! Surround yourself with fellow explorers to add pizzazz to your spiritual quest and reap the benefits of support, encouragement, and accountability.

Think of your spiritual journey as a cosmic road trip. While going solo can be fun, it's even better with a car full of enthusiastic companions! To find your spiritual squad, consider joining a group that aligns with your beliefs or practices. Whether it's a meditation meetup or a secular Buddhist book club, you'll soon find your spiritual GPS re-routing you toward connection and growth.

If you're craving a more immersive experience, spiritual retreats and workshops are where it's at! Swap the concrete jungle for a serene oasis, and dive headfirst into a world of self-discovery and spiritual bonding. You'll forge connections with fellow explorers, learn new skills, and return home armed with a treasure trove of insights.

Don't forget about the digital realm, either! The World Wide Web offers a veritable playground of spiritual communities. Social media platforms, online forums, and blogs are brimming with kindred spirits ready to virtually high-five you on your journey. Just remember to practice discernment in your online engagements—think quality over quantity!

In a nutshell, community is like the secret sauce that spices up your spiritual path. By connecting with like-minded individuals, you'll gain the support, encouragement, and accountability needed to keep trekking onward and upward. So, assemble your spiritual squad and get ready for a soul-enriching adventure like no other!

Get Reflective with Your Inner Guru

Imagine taking a deep dive into the spiritual pool of introspection—welcome to the world of self-reflection! This crucial part of spiritual growth is like having a heart-to-heart with your inner self, and it'll leave you feeling like a spiritual superhero.

Ready to get your reflection on? Journaling is your new BFF. Scribbling down your thoughts and feelings is like turning your brain into a spiritual jukebox, playing the greatest hits of your innermost musings. You'll uncover hidden gems of wisdom and insight, making you the star of your own personal development show.

Meditation is another trusty sidekick on the self-reflection journey. Think of it as a personal timeout in the bustling game of life. Meditation clears the mental clutter, allowing you to tap into your inner voice and soak up the wisdom it has to offer. The result? More self-awareness, clarity, and emotional balance, which basically makes you a spiritual ninja.

But wait, there's more! Contemplative practices like prayer and rituals are like the icing on the self-reflection cake. By creating space for reflection, contemplation, and self-discovery, you're embarking on a spiritual treasure hunt, unearthing nuggets of inner wisdom and deepening your connection to the divine.

In a nutshell, self-reflection is like a spiritual workout, flexing your inner-growth muscles and setting you on the path to spiritual enlightenment. With journaling, meditation, and contemplative practices in your spiritual toolkit, you'll be well on your way to becoming the master of your own spiritual destiny. So, grab a pen, find a quiet spot, and get ready to explore the wonders of your inner world!

Pampering Your Inner Zen Master

Imagine cradling your inner self in a cozy cocoon of love and self-care. Sounds delightful, right? Well, nurturing your inner life is just that—a VIP pass to a meaningful and fulfilling life through the magical world of self-care.

Ready to roll out the red carpet for your inner self? Start by catering to your body's needs. Your body is like your trusty spiritual sidekick, so treat it right with plenty of rest, nutritious noms, and some sweat-inducing exercise. When your body's feeling its best, connecting with your inner self becomes a piece of cake (a healthy one, of course).

Sleep and downtime are the unsung heroes of self-care. Give your body and mind a well-deserved break by catching some Zs and penciling in some chill time. Trust us, your inner Zen master will thank you.

And let's not forget about exercise! Breaking a sweat is like a high-five for your soul. It busts stress, lifts your mood, and energizes you like a double espresso (minus the caffeine jitters). Find your groove, whether it's walking, yoga, or dancing like nobody's watching. Your body (and your inner self) will love you for it.

But wait, there's more to this self-care fiesta! Nurturing your soul through spiritual practices like meditation, journaling, or prayer is like the cherry on top. These soul-boosting activities help you connect with your inner self on a deeper level, turning you into a spiritual powerhouse.

The bottom line: nurturing your inner life is all about showering yourself with love and care. When you make self-care a priority, you'll be well on your way to a life filled with purpose, joy, and meaning. So, go ahead—pamper your inner Zen master and watch your life flourish like never before!

Tackling Spiritual Speed Bumps

So, you've decided to embark on a spiritual journey, but you've hit a few pesky roadblocks along the way? Fear not, spiritual warrior! Doubt, fear, and distraction are like the pesky in-laws of the spiritual world—uninvited but not entirely unwelcome. Embrace the challenge and let's turn those obstacles into opportunities!

Doubt is like that annoying friend who questions everything. It can make us feel like our spiritual compass is spinning out of control. The good news? Doubt is just a pesky thought, and thoughts can be managed. So, when doubt rears its ugly head, take a deep breath, and look for sources of inspiration or guidance from a wise spiritual guru.

Fear is like that big, scary shadow in the corner of the room. But when you turn on the light, it's just a pile of laundry (who knew?). Embrace fear and remind yourself that change is just a part of the spiritual journey. Give yourself a hug, practice self-compassion, and remember that you're a spiritual rockstar in the making.

Now, distraction... oh, look, a squirrel! In our modern world, distraction is as common as cat videos on the internet. But fear not, you can tame this wild beast. Carve out a sacred space for your spiritual practice, set boundaries around your screen time, and show distraction who's boss.

The bottom line: overcoming obstacles is all about self-awareness and intention. Recognize your spiritual speed bumps, and face them head-on with a healthy dose of humor and determination. In the end, you'll emerge with a stronger spiritual practice and a newfound appreciation for the wild ride that is the spiritual journey. So buckle up, buttercup, and let's do this!

Embracing an Attitude of Gratitude

Gratitude is like the magical fairy dust that can transform your spiritual journey, bringing a newfound sense of appreciation for life and a deeper connection to the divine. By practicing gratitude, you can shift your perspective, foster a positive mindset, and enhance your overall spiritual practice.

One way to invite gratitude into your life is through gratitude journaling. Grab a pen and paper, and jot down the things that make your heart sing. By focusing on the good stuff, you'll find that the not-so-good stuff seems to fade into the background. Plus, you'll begin to notice even more reasons to be grateful as you train your brain to seek out the positive.

Another approach to cultivating gratitude is by expressing thanks to the people who make your world go round. Share your appreciation with friends, family, and even strangers. Not only will you brighten their day, but you'll also deepen your connections and create a ripple effect of positivity.

Looking for even more ways to sprinkle gratitude into your spiritual practice? Try incorporating it into your daily meditation, taking a moment to silently give thanks for the blessings in your life. Or simply pause throughout the day to express gratitude for the small moments that bring you joy and contentment.

In conclusion, embracing an attitude of gratitude can have a transformative impact on your spiritual journey. By cultivating appreciation for life's many blessings, you'll foster a deeper connection with the spiritual realm, create a positive mindset, and enrich your overall spiritual experience. So go ahead, give gratitude a whirl, and watch your spiritual practice flourish!

CHAPTER 14

Walking the Talk: Applying Secular Buddhist Philosophy to Daily Life

Grasping Secular Buddhism's Principles: Your Guide to a Zen-er Everyday Life

Enter the world of Secular Buddhism, where ancient teachings collide with modern science to make your life more Zen-tastic. Toss out those old-school concepts like karma and reincarnation, and buckle up for a practical joyride through the principles of Buddhism—no superstitions allowed!

Secular Buddhism revolves around three epic principles: mindfulness, compassion, and wisdom. Mindfulness is like a mental camera, capturing every moment without judgment. Compassion transforms you into an empathy superhero, always looking out for the well-being of others. And wisdom? That's when you realize that everything is as temporary and interconnected as your phone's battery life.

Applying these principles to your daily grind is easier than you think. Mindfulness can turn your stress levels down to zero, sharpen your focus, and clear up that mental fog. Compassion will make you the ultimate BFF, strengthening relationships and making your community a better place. And wisdom? It's like having a life GPS, guiding you toward authentic living, smarter decisions, and a fulfilling existence.

Getting started is a piece of Zen cake. Simply add a sprinkle of meditation, a dash of mindful breathing, and set your daily intentions like you're prepping your morning coffee. Don't forget to practice your empathy skills and reflect on your own biases, because nobody's perfect.

So there you have it: Secular Buddhism—a practical recipe for a more mindful, compassionate, and awesome life. Embrace these principles, and you'll be spreading happiness and well-being like it's going out of style. Namaste!

Mindful Moments: Boost Your Awareness with a Dash of Fun

Mindfulness: It's like adding a pinch of awesomesauce to your daily routine. You'll be more present, less stressed, and super-charged with well-being. Ready to amp up your awareness of thoughts, emotions, and behaviors? Here's your quick and quirky guide to living in the now:

Schedule a mindfulness date with yourself. Just five to ten minutes a day is all it takes to kickstart your journey. Soon, you'll be the master of your Zen domain!

Find your Zen den. Whether it's your closet or your favorite armchair, pick a spot that's quiet, comfy, and free from distractions. Set an "I'm in my happy place" vibe.

Breathe like a boss. Tune into the sensation of air flowing in and out of your lungs. When your mind wanders off to la-la land, kindly escort it back to your breath.

Observe your inner landscape. Watch your thoughts, emotions, and behaviors as if you were the star of your own reality show. No judgments, just curiosity and compassion.

Embrace the good, the bad, and the ugly. Instead of running from tricky thoughts or emotions, welcome them like unexpected party guests. You'll learn a thing or two about yourself in the process.

Make mindfulness your daily sidekick. Whether you're scrubbing dishes or singing in the shower, invite mindfulness along for the ride. Watch your day transform into a sensory feast!

Get your groove on with guided meditations and apps. There's no shame in seeking a little digital support to boost your mindfulness game.

So there you have it—mindfulness practices, with a twist of fun! Infuse your life with these tips, and you'll be on your way to a more aware, peaceful, and downright fantastic existence. Happy mindful living!

Peaceful Vibes: Meditation Hacks for a Chill Life

Stressed out? Overwhelmed? Sounds like you need a meditation vacation! Our busy lives can leave our minds feeling like a tangled mess, but with a little Zen magic, you'll be floating on cloud nine in no time. Let's dive into the world of meditation techniques to help you chillax and find your inner bliss.

Set the stage for Zen-tastic meditation. Locate a quiet corner where you can escape the hustle and bustle. Get cozy, sit up straight, and let the relaxation begin.

Breathe like a cool cucumber. Inhale deeply and feel the air fill your lungs, then exhale as if you're blowing away your worries. Remember, thoughts are like party crashers—acknowledge them, but gently show them the door.

Count your breaths like a Zen master. Keep track of each inhale and exhale, and watch your focus skyrocket. Start with a few minutes, then work your way up to full-on meditation marathons.

Let guided meditation be your spirit guide. Pop in some earbuds and let a soothing voice whisk you away to a land of tranquility. New to meditation? Guided sessions are like training wheels for your Zen journey.

The secret to meditation? Keep it simple and stress-free. A few minutes a day can transform your life into a stress-busting, peace-loving adventure. So go on, meditate your way to a happier, more zen-tastic you! Namaste, friend!

Unleash Your Inner Kindness Ninja: Daily Compassion Hacks

Ready to become a kindness ninja, spreading warm fuzzies wherever you go? Compassion and kindness are like secret weapons, turning everyday interactions into heartwarming moments. Remember, everyone's facing their own challenges, and your kindness could be the highlight of their day.

Time to kick your kindness skills up a notch with these daily compassion hacks:

Mindful chit-chat: Next time you're conversing with someone, hit the pause button on autopilot mode. Tune in, actively listen, and empathize with their story. You'll be amazed at the connections you'll make.

Kindness in action: Channel your inner kindness superhero with small but mighty gestures. Hold doors open, flash a smile, or lend a helping hand. You never know whose day you'll brighten with these tiny acts of awesomeness.

Gratitude galore: Make appreciation your daily mantra. Celebrate the goodness in your life and the people who bring it. A grateful heart is a magnet for kindness and positive vibes.

Ready to change the world with compassion and kindness? Practice these hacks in your daily interactions, and you'll create a kindness ripple effect that knows no bounds. Time to unleash your inner kindness ninja!

Embrace the Ephemeral: Life Lessons in Letting Go

Ready for a ride on the roller coaster of life? The truth is, everything's here one moment and gone the next. But don't despair—embrace the fleeting nature of it all, and you'll unlock the secret to a life of freedom and happiness.

Time to level up your letting-go game with these tips for releasing attachments and ditching the cling:

Identify your happiness hitchhikers: We all have those sneaky attachments—material things, relationships, experiences, or even our own identities—that we think we need to be happy. Spoiler alert: happiness is an inside job!

Detach and declutter: Time to let go of those happiness hitchhikers. When things inevitably change or vanish, you'll be ready to roll with the punches, knowing that your happiness isn't tied to them.

Unstick from the past: Clinging to old grudges or bygone relationships? Break free and make room for new adventures and connections.

Befriend the present: Embrace the now, savoring each moment like a fine wine. No worrying about the future or dwelling on the past—just pure, unfiltered presence.

Flex your resilience muscles: When you let go of attachments and clinging, you become a master of adaptation. Life's curveballs? No problem—you've got this!

Practice makes perfect, so be patient with yourself as you learn to let go. Try mindfulness techniques like meditation to help you embrace life's impermanence. The result? Greater peace, joy, and a newfound love for the ever-changing adventure we call life.

Become a Zen Master: Tips for Practicing Non-Judgment and Non-Reactivity

Want to stay cool, calm, and collected, no matter what life throws at you? Practicing non-judgment and non-reactivity can help you keep your emotional balance and navigate life's surprises with ease. Here's how to become a Zen master in the face of external triggers:

Thought-wrangling 101: Monitor those sneaky, critical thoughts that pop up. Challenge them and ask if they're truly accurate or helpful. Remember, you're the boss of your thoughts!

Press the pause button: When faced with challenging situations, hit pause and take a few deep breaths. Give yourself time to recalibrate before responding—think of it as an emotional reset.

Emotion-watching: Pretend you're a curious observer, watching your emotions as they come and go. By detaching from them, you'll be better equipped to handle life's ups and downs.

Breathe, baby, breathe: When you feel overwhelmed or reactive, take a few moments to focus on your breath, sensations, or surroundings. Let the breath be your anchor in the storm.

Self-care like a pro: Prioritize activities that make you feel awesome—hobbies, exercise, meditation, or spending time with loved ones. When you nurture yourself, you build resilience and strength to handle life's curveballs.

By following these tips, you'll be on your way to cultivating non-judgment and non-reactivity, empowering you to navigate life's challenges with grace and poise. Go forth and conquer, Zen master!

Channeling Your Inner Ethical Superhero: Secular Buddhism's Take on Ethics and Morality

In a world where superheroes dominate the box office, it's time to unleash your inner ethical superhero with the help of secular Buddhism! This modern take on Buddhist teachings emphasizes ethical principles and practical wisdom, rather than religious dogma, making it perfect for today's morally-conscious world.

Ready to don your cape and save the day? Let's dive into the secular Buddhist philosophy of ethics and morality, and how it can help you make better decisions and conduct yourself like a true hero:

Embrace the Four Noble Truths: These nuggets of wisdom teach us that suffering exists, it's caused by craving, and can be overcome by letting go of cravings. The ultimate guide to conquering suffering? The Eightfold Path, of course!

Walk the Eightfold Path: This ethical roadmap includes Right Speech, Right Action, and Right Livelihood, inspiring us to be compassionate, honest, nonviolent, and respectful to all living beings. No cape needed!

Mindfulness and meditation to the rescue: Develop your ethical superpowers through mindfulness and meditation practices. This will help you gain insight, wisdom, and a more compassionate way of being in the world.

Channel your inner superhero: When faced with decisions, consider how your choices will affect yourself and others, whether they align with your values and ethical principles, and if there are kinder, more compassionate alternatives.

By applying secular Buddhist ethical principles to your personal conduct and decision-making, you'll not only be a hero to yourself and others but also contribute to a more just and compassionate world. So go on, unleash your inner ethical superhero, and make the world a better place—one kind act at a time!

CHAPTER 15

Doing the Right Thing: Living a Morally Responsible and Ethical Life with Secular Buddhism

The Art of Living an Ethically Hilarious and Morally Witty Life

Embarking on the journey of living a morally responsible and ethical life is like attempting to balance a cup of tea on your head while walking on a tightrope. It's all about making decisions and taking actions that jive with your values and principles. Imagine you're a stand-up comedian, and your punchlines are acts of kindness, respect, honesty, and integrity—now that's a performance worth watching!

In this wacky world, living an ethically groovy life means being mindful of the ripple effect your actions create. Picture yourself as a human boomerang—whatever you do comes back to you in one form or another. So, make choices that benefit not only you but also your fellow humans and the environment. After all, we're all in this cosmic sitcom together.

Think of being ethical as having a moral GPS that guides you on the path of awesomeness. It's like having a built-in laugh track that only plays when you avoid harmful actions, treat others fairly, and remain transparent and honest in your dealings. Who wouldn't want that?

Living an ethically amusing life demands constant self-reflection and a dash of humor. It's like watching reruns of your life and learning from the bloopers. Embrace your inner Buddha and commit to personal growth. Laugh at your mistakes, and let them be the stepping stones toward living in harmony with your values and principles.

In the grand cosmic joke that is life, living a morally responsible and ethical existence will lead you to a sense of purpose and fulfillment. It's like being the star of your own feel-good movie, where you spread joy, compassion, and dignity. So, grab your popcorn, sit back, and enjoy the ride!

The Hilarious Perks of Living a Morally Upright and Ethically Comedic Life

Embrace the chuckles and grins that come with living a morally responsible and ethical life, and you'll soon discover a treasure trove of benefits. Let's take a stroll down the side-splitting path of moral responsibility, shall we?

Inner peace: Picture yourself snoozing on a cloud of guilt-free tranquility. By not intentionally harming others, your conscience becomes your fluffy bedtime companion, granting you nights filled with sweet dreams.

Better relationships: Just like a magnet attracts metal, an ethical life lures in folks who share your values. The result? A joyous jamboree of meaningful and positive connections. Friendship goals, anyone?

Trustworthy: Consistently living a morally responsible and ethical life transforms you into a trusty sidekick, opening doors to exciting career escapades and deepening personal bonds. Who doesn't want to be a superhero's best buddy?

Self-improvement: Striving to live an ethical life is like doing mental push-ups – the more you do, the stronger you get. Flex those self-improvement muscles and watch your personal growth skyrocket!

Helping others: Choosing the path of moral responsibility and ethical behavior is like being a stand-up comedian for the soul. Your positive impact on others can lead to a sense of fulfillment and purpose that's more satisfying than the perfect punchline.

Good Reputation: Picture yourself wearing a sparkling crown of ethical awesomeness. By living a morally responsible life, you'll build a reputation that shines, earning the respect and admiration of your adoring audience.

So, giggle your way to greatness by living a morally responsible and ethical life.

Not only will you feel fantastic, but you'll also enjoy the side-splitting benefits of improved relationships, career opportunities, and a sense of purpose. With laughter as your guide, personal growth and fulfillment are just a chuckle away.

Navigating the Comedy of Errors: Spotting Moral and Ethical Dilemmas with a Chuckle

Moral and ethical dilemmas are like a comedic duel between two equally matched jokesters, each trying to outwit the other. These situations pit conflicting values against each other, causing a mental tug-of-war that makes you question which punchline to choose. Identifying moral and ethical dilemmas is essential for living a life that's both upright and uproarious.

Here's how to spot moral and ethical dilemmas with a wink and a smile:

Appreciate your inner moral comedian: Acknowledge the importance of moral and ethical values in your life. They're the zingers that make your life's performance a hit.

Sniff out the tough calls: You've found a dilemma when your moral compass spins like a propeller. For example, choosing between spilling the beans or keeping a secret to protect someone.

Ponder the punchlines: Dilemmas often pop up when the implications of your actions are uncertain or conflicting. Think about the short-term and long- term effects of your potential choices.

Consult the comedy rulebook: In professional settings, ethical codes can be your gag guide, helping you navigate tricky dilemmas with finesse.

Ask the audience: Seek advice from trusted friends or colleagues to gain different perspectives on the dilemma. They might just help you find the perfect one-liner.

Evaluate your comedic style: Reflect on your values and beliefs to figure out why you're caught in a dilemma. This introspection will help you land on a decision that aligns with your unique brand of humor.

In a nutshell, spotting moral and ethical dilemmas means understanding the guiding principles that make you the star of your own comedy show. By considering the implications of your choices and seeking input from others, you can make decisions that stay true to your values and keep your audience laughing.

Humorous Tactics for Tackling Tricky Moral and Ethical Conundrums

Navigating the twists and turns of difficult moral and ethical decisions can feel like trying to juggle flaming torches while riding a unicycle. But fear not! These comedic strategies will help you keep your balance and find the perfect punchline:

Do your homework: Gather intel on the issue like a stand-up comedian scouting for new material. Consult articles, ask opinions from trusty sidekicks, and learn from others' experiences. Knowledge is power, and it'll help you deliver the right zinger.

Unearth your comedic core: Dig deep and identify your fundamental values and principles. Reflect on your beliefs, goals, and priorities. This self-awareness will help you make decisions that keep your performance on point and your inner conflict at bay.

Weigh the punchlines: Put on your thinking cap and ponder the potential consequences of each option. Think about how your decision will impact others – after all, the best comedians know how to work a crowd.

Phone a friend: Seek counsel from your trusty advisors, whether they're family, friends, mentors, or professionals. Discuss various alternatives, evaluate pros and cons, and consider their input while making your decision.

Bust your biases: Take a good look at your biases and preconceptions, then give them the boot. Recognizing and challenging your biases will help you make a decision that's based on truth, not assumptions.

Ponder the big picture: When making a moral or ethical decision, don't forget to consider the long-term effects on your life and those around you. After all, it's the punchlines that leave a lasting impression that count.

Tune in to your inner comedian: Trust your gut, moral instincts, and conscience. Let your internal comedy radar guide you to make the right decision, even when it's not the easiest path.

In the end, making challenging moral and ethical decisions is no laughing matter. It takes a clear mind, an open heart, and the courage to act according to your values. With these strategies in your comedic toolkit, you'll be well-equipped to make informed decisions that align with your moral compass and conscience, leaving your audience in stitches.

Lights, Camera, Action: Broadcasting Your Moral and Ethical Beliefs with Humor

Communicating your moral and ethical beliefs can feel like performing a stand-up routine for the toughest crowd. But fear not! With these tips, you'll have your audience in stitches while imparting your values:

Get up close and personal: Before taking center stage, be crystal clear about your moral and ethical beliefs. Reflect on your values and jot them down, so you can deliver your performance with panache.

Lend an ear: To create a respectful banter, pay attention to your audience's thoughts about your beliefs. Understand their concerns, weave them into your script, and adjust your message accordingly.

Tell a tale: When sharing your moral and ethical beliefs, use anecdotes and examples to make your point relatable and engaging. After all, everyone loves a good story with a punchline.

Mind your manners: While expressing your values, respect others' opinions, even if they clash with yours. Keep judgments and criticism at bay for a harmonious exchange.

Welcome the hecklers: People may throw questions or doubts your way regarding your beliefs. Embrace them, address their concerns honestly, and clear up any misconceptions with a wink and a smile.

Bring you're a-game: When delivering your beliefs, exude confidence and conviction. Your audience will be more likely to trust your message if they see you're fully committed to your script.

To sum up, effectively communicating your moral and ethical beliefs is like mastering the art of stand-up comedy. By understanding yourself, using anecdotes, respecting others, being open to questions, and speaking confidently, you'll have your audience laughing and learning along with you.

Morals, Ethics, and Society: Riding the Cultural Roller Coaster

Social and cultural influences can make navigating the world of morals and ethics feel like a roller coaster ride, with unexpected twists and turns at every corner. Let's buckle up and explore some of these influential elements that shape our moral and ethical behavior:

Religion: The Divine Comedy

Religion plays a significant role in shaping our moral and ethical beliefs, offering divine guidance on how to distinguish between right and wrong.

While each religion has its own unique moral compass, they all seek to steer their followers toward ethical living.

Family: The Ethics Factory

The family is where we first learn the difference between good and bad behavior. Our parents become our moral and ethical superheroes, teaching us the ways of the ethical force, and modeling values we carry with us throughout life.

Education: The School of Morals

From kindergarten to university, education influences our moral and ethical behavior, providing us with the tools we need to make informed decisions. Classrooms become laboratories, where students experiment with ethical theories and learn about the impact of their actions.

Media: The Morality Megaphone

The media can be a double-edged sword when it comes to shaping moral and ethical behavior. On one hand, it can promote positive values, but on the other, it can glorify unethical actions. As consumers, we must be discerning in what we expose ourselves to, filtering out the "bad apples" from the "good fruit."

Culture: The Ethics Buffet

Cultural influences can be a smorgasbord of varying beliefs and behaviors, each with its own unique flavor. While some cultural norms can promote ethical behavior, others can challenge our own moral values. It's essential to be aware of these differences and respect them, even if we don't always agree.

In conclusion, navigating the roller coaster of social and cultural influences on moral and ethical behavior requires a keen sense of awareness and adaptability. By being proactive and striving for ethical values through positive reinforcement and education, we can contribute to shaping a more moral and ethical society for generations to come. So, hold on tight and enjoy the ride!

Boost Your Ethical IQ: Top Resources for Moral and Ethical Enlightenment

Ready to flex your moral muscles and elevate your ethical expertise? Check out these fantastic resources that can help you achieve the ethical six-pack you've been dreaming of:

1. Ethics Resource Center (ERC) - The ERC is your one-stop-shop for all things ethics, providing a treasure trove of tools and resources to promote ethical decision-making. Whether you're after consulting services or research studies, they've got you covered.

2. The Markkula Center for Applied Ethics - Consider this center your personal ethics coach, with a vast array of resources to help you flex your moral muscles. Get inspired by case studies, articles, and podcasts that will have you pondering profound ethical questions.

3. Ethics Unwrapped - Brought to you by the University of Texas at Austin, this online program offers binge-worthy video content to help you understand real-world ethical conundrums. Netflix, who?

4. Institute for Global Ethics (IGE) - This worldwide ethical powerhouse offers training and resources to transform individuals and organizations into ethics superheroes. Get ready to save the world, one ethical decision at a time!

5. The Josephson Institute of Ethics - This altruistic organization provides all the ethical training and resources you need to become a moral mastermind. Discover interactive workshops, articles, and multimedia content that will make you an ethics aficionado in no time.

6. Ethics.org - Your go-to destination for all things ethics on the world wide web. Find news articles, podcasts, and a directory of ethical resources that will keep you informed and engaged.

7. Ethics and Compliance Initiative (ECI) - ECI is your ethical personal trainer, providing research, best practices, and training to help organizations develop ethical cultures. Whip your ethics into shape with their case studies, webinars, and white papers.

8. National Association of State Boards of Accountancy (NASBA) – NASBA offers professional development courses that help accountants to understand, identify and respond to ethical issues. They also offer resources to help accountants to maintain ethical standards and fulfill professional ethics requirements.

9. National Association of Corporate Directors (NACD) – NACD provides resources and training to corporate directors to enable them to demonstrate ethical leadership, which is a critical element in the success of organizations.

10. CharacterFirst Education - This nonprofit organization provides character education resources for teachers and parents. Their materials help students develop ethical leadership skills, self-discipline, and emotional intelligence.

11. Your MORAL Compass App – This handy iPhone app will be your ethical sidekick, helping you evaluate ethical dilemmas and guiding you through the decision-making process. Ethical enlightenment, right at your fingertips!

12. EthicsGame - Level up your ethical prowess with this educational program offering a range of games and simulations. Suitable for all ages and available in both classroom and online learning environments, EthicsGame is the ultimate way to boost your ethical IQ.

With these fantastic resources in your ethical arsenal, you'll be well on your way to becoming a moral and ethical champion!

A FINAL NOTE:
GO FORTH AND BE MINDFUL

Well, folks, we've reached the end of our journey together. It's been a wild ride, full of laughs, insights, and more than a few "aha!" moments. But now it's time to say goodbye.

Before we part ways, though, I want to leave you with a final thought. It's a simple one, but one that I believe is crucial to living a fulfilling life. Are you ready for it?

Be mindful.

That's it. Just be mindful. Easy, right?

Of course, it's not really that easy. Mindfulness takes practice, patience, and a willingness to be present in the moment. But it's worth it. Trust me.

When you're mindful, you're more aware of your thoughts, feelings, and surroundings. You're less likely to get caught up in the past or the future, and more likely to appreciate the beauty of the present moment.

You're also more likely to be kinder, more compassionate, and more understanding. When you're mindful, you're less reactive and more responsive. You're less likely to fly off the handle when someone cuts you off in traffic or forgets to return your text message, and more likely to respond with grace and kindness.

And that's what it's all about, my friends. Being mindful isn't just good for you; it's good for everyone around you. It's like a ripple effect. When you're more mindful, you inspire others to be more mindful too. And before you know it, we've created a world that's a little kinder, a little more compassionate, and a little more understanding.

So go forth, my friends, and be mindful. Practice mindfulness in everything you do, from brushing your teeth to having a conversation with a loved one. And remember, even when you slip up (which you will, because you're human), that's okay. Mindfulness is a practice, not a destination.

Thank you for joining me on this journey of exploration and personal growth. I hope you've found this book to be informative, entertaining, and maybe even a little bit inspiring. And always remember: when in doubt, be mindful.

Thank you!

Your friend,

ABOUT THE AUTHOR

Alright, folks, let's talk about the man behind the book. We're talking about a best-selling author, professional keynote speaker, and publishing, speaking, and marketing coach. That's right, John Webster is a jack of all trades.

Now, you might think this guy had a cushy job lined up right out of college. But nope, John decided to live life on his own terms and embrace the entrepreneurial lifestyle. He's been at it for thirty years now, and let's just say he's learned a thing or two about leadership, change, time management, financial wealth, and achieving your dreams.

Oh, and did we mention he's from Texas? That's right, John's a true cowboy at heart. But he traded in his spurs for some desert boots and now lives in Arizona with his lovely wife, Melissa.

So if you're feeling lost and don't know where to turn, don't worry. John's got your back. He's here to help you master your fate and achieve more time, money, freedom, health, love, and happiness. You know, just the small stuff.

ABOUT PUBLISHING COACHING

Alright, folks, it's time to get serious. We're talking about the secret to standing out from your competition, boosting your profits, and becoming a superstar in your field. And what's the secret, you ask? It's writing and publishing a book, baby!

That's right, a published book is like a lead-generating machine that helps you attract clients, secure speaking gigs, and rake in the dough. And who better to guide you through the process than John Webster? This guy's a professional speaker, publishing coach, and marketing coach all rolled into one.

Don't worry if you're feeling overwhelmed. John's got your back. He'll be your coach for life, guiding you through every step of the process, from writing your book to marketing it like a boss. And if you're worried about the cost, don't be. John's here to save you both time and money.

Plus, he's mentored over 1,000 clients, so you know he's the real deal. So go ahead, check out his websites, and then shoot him a text. He'll set you up with a complimentary coaching consultation by phone or Zoom. You won't regret it!

So what are you waiting for? It's time to become a published author and take your career to the next level. John Webster is ready and waiting to help you make it happen.

www.CoachJohnWebster.com
480-500-8500

BOOK JOHN WEBSTER TO SPEAK AT YOUR NEXT EVENT

Are you tired of boring speakers who put you to sleep faster than a lullaby? Well, have no fear, John Webster is here! This guy's the real deal when it comes to professional speaking.

With over 1,200 presentations under his belt, John's got the skills to pay the bills. Whether you've got ten people or 5,000, he can deliver a customized message of faith, hope, and inspiration that'll leave your audience begging for more.

And forget about those stuffy lectures. John's not here to "teach" anyone anything. He's all about storytelling, baby. He'll amuse your audience with tales of triumph over adversity, leaving them feeling inspired and ready to take on the world.

Oh, and did we mention he's hilarious? That's right, folks, you'll be laughing so hard you'll forget you're actually learning something.

So if you're looking for a speaker who'll leave a lasting impression, look no further than John Webster. Check out his website, watch his highlight reel, and then give him a call or shoot him an text or email. He'll even do a complimentary pre-speech phone interview to make sure he's the right fit for your event. Trust us, folks, John's the man for the job.

www.CoachJohnWebster.com
480-500-8500

www.ingramcontent.com/pod-product-compliance
Lightning Source LLC
La Vergne TN
LVHW010657110826
845149LV00014B/3139

9781962043076